TRUTH
AND
LOVE

♀♂⚢⚣⚤ IN A SEXUALLY
DISORDERED WORLD

'Here is wisdom, factual , medical and biblical to guide our thinking about our sexuality and especially about homosexual practice; here too is fuel for our compassion and prayers.'

Ann Allen

'In a day when there is such confusion on matters of human sexuality, we need a clear biblical exposition of the issues. This is it!'

Peter Maiden, International Director of OM

'One of the best books available on this highly important subject. Balanced, biblical and readable, it is urgently necessary in the contemporary confusion of our culture. I hope it is widely read.'

Eric Alexander

'A biblical and pastoral approach to the whole issue of sexuality... the contemporary battleground for the soul of the church.'

Philip Hacking

TRUTH
AND
LOVE

♀♂⚦⚥⚧ IN A SEXUALLY
DISORDERED WORLD

EDITED BY **DAVID SEARLE**

CHRISTIAN FOCUS

Copyright © David C Searle

ISBN 1-84550-227-2
ISBN 978-1-84550-227-0

10 9 8 7 6 5 4 3 2 1

First Published 1996
by Paternoster Publishing
This Revised Edition Published in 2006
by
Christian Focus Publications, Ltd.,
Geanies House, Fearn, Ross-shire
IV20 1TW, United Kingdom

www.christianfocus.com

Printed by
Nørhaven Paperback A/S

Typeset by David C Searle, Arbroath
Cover Design by Moose77.com

Contents

Acknowledgements

I am grateful to Mrs Alison Carter for proof-reading the Introduction, Epilogue and Chapters 1 to 7. Time restrictions in preparing the text for publication made it impossible for her to proof-read the remainder and any errors in either typesetting, punctuation or spelling are entirely my responsibility.

I must also acknowledge my personal debt to several resources of which I made use in writing Chapters 1 and 7: Henri Blocher's excellent commentary on Genesis 1–3, *In the Beginning* (pub. IVP, Leicester, 1984), John Calvin's commentary on *Genesis* (edition used pub. Banner of Truth, Edinburgh, 1965), and Martyn Lloyd-Jones on Ephesians 5, *Life in the Spirit in Marriage, Home and Work* (pub. Banner of Truth, Edinburgh, 1974). Readers who are familiar with any of these works will at once recognize my dependence on them.

My gratitude must be expressed to Dr Trevor Stammers who prepared the material for Chapter 8 at very short notice, and who himself checked the very full Endnotes; also to Professor David Wright and Rutherford House who readily gave me their permission to use a shortened version of David's original booklet as Chapter 9. I am also grateful to Christian Focus Publications for their co-operation and for their willingness to republish this little book.

DCS

Foreword

You may ask, 'Why a book on *truth and love*? Who needs that?'

The answer is, more of us than one might think! Because the truth is, those of us living in the multicultural, pluralistic culture of the west are increasingly confused about sex, morality and personal identity.

It's not surprising, really, given the melting-pot of competing ideologies that surround us today. The voices are so strong and penetrating—especially in the all-powerful media—that Christians, as well as everyone else, inevitably absorb these messages into their thinking. Subtly, and perhaps almost unconsciously, our views are gradually shaped and moulded as the world around us changes. Old certainties are undermined, replaced by the shifting sands of relativism. Our confidence in what we *think* we think, becomes shaky.

On the public stage, politicians continue to erode the unique status of marriage in society. They undervalue the place of loving, dutiful motherhood and responsible, committed fatherhood as the rock on which solid family life is built, and stable communities flourish.

No doubt it is meant well, trying to address the tragic fact of tens of thousands of single parents struggling to cope alone with their families. But devaluing marriage to 'level the playing field' for all is hardly the answer. The tragic epidemic (it may soon be the majority) of children growing up without one or other of their parents will not be solved this way.

We must face the facts: the widespread confusion surrounding our closest relationships is one chief cause of major societal problems throughout the western world.

But where do we turn for answers? There are few voices willing to suggest that the morality which has been the anchorage of our civilisation for many centuries may have something to offer after all. Pope Benedict XVI has spoken out fearlessly; but outside the Roman Catholic Church, how many are listening to him?

We all know that when struggling to build flatpack furniture successfully, the only way to avoid confusion and disaster is to consult and follow the maker's instructions. Building sexual relationships successfully is a subject of far greater importance—for every human being, and every human society. Sex is a wonderful and exciting gift from God himself, and we are right to celebrate it. But handled wrongly, it is both dangerous and destructive. It can, and does, go terribly wrong.

An alternative title for this book might have been: *Sex—handle with care!* Sex has brought immense happiness to countless millions. But it has also dealt sorrow and heartache to just as many. It need not, and it should not; hence this little book. In it the contributors present lucidly, and without need for apology, our Maker's instructions on how to handle one of the most wonderful gifts he has given to us—our human sexuality. If we will trust *his* guidance, we shall find it really is the way to lasting fulfilment and greatest joy.

Dr William J U Philip

Introduction

After centuries of neglecting the problems that arise from our human sexuality in the vain hope that these problems will somehow go away if we ignore them, it is surely right and proper that Christians today should be urgently addressing them. However, it is clearly important that the method we adopt must be both appropriate and valid. Otherwise, any conclusions will be flawed, and the problems on which we have worked to throw light will be as clouded as they have been in the past.

There are two possible approaches to problems associated with our human sexuality. One way of proceeding might be to begin with an investigation of what people who are affected by such problems themselves feel and think. From there, the expertise of those who have sought to work with them in a supportive role could be tapped. In this way, up-to-date thinking would become available for those seeking to come to terms with sexual problems.

But grave doubts must hang over this method of working. The opinions of any section of contemporary society are bound to be as shifting as the pattern left on the sand by the ebbing tide. Truth itself becomes relative, and accommodates itself to the current vogue in any culture's thinking. An alternative approach must therefore be sought.

Christians believe, and those ordained to positions of leadership in virtually every Christian denomination and fellowship avow, that Scripture is the final source of authority in all matters of faith and conduct. Our method, therefore, must be to seek to assess as accurately and fairly as possible, what the Bible says on all problems which arise from our human sexuality. This will at least give us a starting point from which to work, and a basis for our endeavours to provide pastoral love and care, and full acceptance into Christian fellowship of those who in the past may have felt excluded.

When we begin with Scripture, we at once discover that every living person has departed in thought and motive from the will of God in sexual behaviour, and since none is righteous in this area of living, there is no room for censorious attitudes. Dr Merville Vincent (quoted in John Stott's *Issues Facing Christians Today*, p. 302) says: 'In God's view I suspect we are all sexual deviants. I doubt if there is anyone who has not had a lustful thought that deviated from God's perfect ideal of sexuality.'

To uphold the standards of sexuality given in the Bible could be costly for any Christian church in her relationship to today's society. For standards are changing so rapidly that many of the younger generation no longer are aware that Christians believe God has provided clear standards for our sexuality. But unless the church is to be influenced by society, instead of herself acting as salt and light in society, we Christians must not shrink from such distinctiveness, nor from the possible adverse response which may result. The light must be put on its stand; the city must continue to be seen standing high on the hill.

There is one obvious difference between starting with the way things are at present—how people think and behave—and starting with the Bible. The Bible starts with heterosexuality, and assumes it throughout, not with sexuality in a non-specific sense; whereas it is common today for discussion to begin with an indeterminate sexuality and only then to consider its different expressions. The Christian Scriptures know nothing of a floating sexual identity which may issue in a range of different sexual actions. Its basis throughout is unambiguously heterosexual —man and woman created sexually for each other. While Christians must always be sensitive to what is happening in society, it is crucial that we do not adopt a starting point which in this case would effectively silence the Bible's main voice and message on the issue.

In the following pages, various aspects of sexuality are dealt with. But whether the treatment explains biblical teaching (as in chapters 1 and 7) or applies that teaching to contemporary society (as in chapters 2, 3 and 9) or deals pastorally with personal issues (as in chapters 4, 5 and 6), the starting point is always Scripture. For our firm conviction is that God has spoken fully and finally in and through his Son, Jesus Christ. Using the Christian Scriptures as the starting point, each contributor seeks to show the relevance for today of orthodox Christian morality. How successful this endeavour has been will be measured by the usefulness of this book.

DCS

Chapter One

Sexuality in Genesis 1 and 2

David C. Searle

As we approach the subject of sexuality, we are aware of two extreme attitudes common today in any discussion of it.

First, there is the Victorian reluctance to speak candidly at all about sexuality: this was a subject that was taboo. Many today accuse the Victorians of hypocrisy and allege that beneath the cloak of silence were concealed repression and even cruelty. (Though there is undoubtedly truth in this charge, one has to remember that many Victorian homes were happy and balanced, the women there honoured, fulfilled and given worthy status.)

Second, there is the opposite extreme of complete openness. The brilliant writer, D. H. Lawrence, breached the 19th century dam of secrecy, but the result has been that readiness to speak more openly about sexuality has led to a deluge of shameless exploitation. We are now invaded by an eroticism—almost a deification of sex—which has run out of control.

When we turn to the biblical treatment of sexuality, we find a careful balance between these two extremes. While sexuality is spoken of with candour and honesty, it is nevertheless seen as a sacred gift of God not to be regarded with careless familiarity. In Genesis chapters 1 and 2, we find neither Victorian prudery nor our modern shameless obsession with sex. Rather, sexuality is dealt with in language which is both beautiful and disciplined. However, the church today often fails to reflect this biblical balance and unfortunately the old Victorian attitudes are at times still reflected among many Christians.

Researching pre-biblical writings on this same subject is like wandering across the moors looking for water: there are plenty of pools, but they are all muddied or stagnant, until one suddenly comes upon a pool, unlike the rest, where the water is clean and uncontaminated. That pool is the Genesis treatment of sexuality. The pool is so clear that one's reflection can easily be seen in its pure waters.

But the Genesis tablets are unique in another way. They lay the basis for the Bible's

whole thinking and teaching on this subject of
sexuality. When Luther wrote that the early
chapters of Genesis were foundational for all
biblical theology, sexuality was certainly
included.

The likeness of man and woman

> Then God said, 'Let us make man in our
> image, in our likeness...'. So God created
> man in his own image... male and female he
> created them (Genesis 1:26f.).

Twice over, the word *man* is used in a
common sense of both male and female. We
might even (as the NRSV has done) translate
man here by 'humankind'. This common
meaning of the noun *man* is rapidly being lost,
and many have assumed that there is a built-
in male bias here.

Not so; the use of the noun *man* for both
male and female is emphasizing their *likeness*. It
is laying down the principle that the man and
the woman stand side by side as equals,
distinct and apart from everything else God
has made ('let them rule over the fish of the
sea and the birds in the air, over the livestock,
over all the earth, and over all the creatures
that move along the ground' [1:26b]), with
their very being as living souls (2:7, AV) the

great common aspect of their existence. They are created standing side by side as equals.

The detail about the *rib* (2:21f.) teaches the same principle. There are at least three possible understandings of *tsela* (the rib). (i) It can be translated as 'side' (so NIV margin). This meaning underlines the 'side-by-sideness' of the man and the woman. We have in English a similar saying in the phrase, 'my other half'. (ii) A second meaning comes from Arabic where it means 'my closest friend' in the sense of one who is at my very side and without whom I cannot do. (iii) A third possible meaning comes from Sumerian where it means 'life'. In 3:20 we are told that Adam calls his wife 'Eve' meaning 'life'. Probably the best translation is (i), that is, 'side'. The force of the idea of the woman coming from the man's side is that they make a perfect pair in their side-by-sideness. It is emphasizing their likeness.

There is yet another aspect of the pair's likeness: it comes first in their joint relationship to God as created in his likeness. God created them in his image, first and foremost, an equal pair, a pair of equals. If they are honest, men have to make the confession that equality has often been violated down the ages. Repeatedly, the balance has been lost. We should note at this point two distortions in thinking about sexuality which have come to us through men's transgression against women's equality.

The first is the unbiblical 'macho' image of the man, which is both foolish and arrogant. The Psalms tell us plainly that God takes no pleasure in that kind of male image (Psalm 147:10). Experience teaches us that men acting the macho image make bad husbands and worse lovers. Women prefer men to be thoughtful, considerate, gentle and loving. The macho male distortion roughly sets to one side the woman's equality with the man.

The second distortion arising from this neglect of the equality between the sexes is the false concept of the eternal femininity on the one hand, and the reading of 'maleness' into God's nature on the other hand. The error of the concept of eternal femininity is that it introduces sexuality into the Godhead; likewise, it is a misunderstanding of Deity to read maleness into the fatherhood of God. Genesis 1:26f. is not saying that God made the male in his own image and likeness. *Man* made in the image of God (that is, *male and female* created in the divine image) is stressing that in the likeness of the man and the woman to each other they are made in God's image and likeness. In other words, an important aspect of the image of God in humankind is the fundamental likeness of male and female to each other. If we make God either male or female, we drive a horse and carriage through that likeness, and embark on the foolish and vain endeavour to build a relationship with God on the basis of sexuality and male-female differentiation.

Reproduction, as we know it, requires both male and female. But God creates; he does not reproduce. Though Scripture thinks anthropomorphically about God, using both paternal and maternal concepts (e.g., Luke 15:11ff. and Matthew 23:37), it is misleading and inaccurate to ascribe sexuality to God.

The difference between man and woman

In Genesis 1, God is represented as reviewing what he has done six times over and seeing that it is good. But in 2:18 there is a significant statement of something that is not good, and this means there is something still to be done:

> The Lord God said, 'It is not good for the man to be alone. I will make a helper suitable for him.'

And so came the woman, equal to the man, but yet different from him. That is the principle being established here. Male and female are not the same. They are essentially different, and the woman's femininity permeates her being (though her equality must not be sacrificed to that femininity).

There is a strong modern belief that, granted certain necessary anatomical and physiological differences between the sexes, men and women are essentially the same. Any differences which develop during childhood are only the result of environmental conditioning. But Genesis 2 is teaching there is an intended difference between the sexes: 'I will make a helper suitable for him', translated in NRSV: 'I will make him a helper as his partner'.

The word *helper* speaks of co-operation, not rivalry, because it was complementarity that was God's will for the man and woman. Some women have objected to the word 'helper' as being both derogatory and patronizing. But this word is used only 21 times in the Old Testament, and 15 of those occurrences describe God as our Helper, lifting up broken, defeated and helpless men, setting them on their feet and encouraging and strengthening them (e.g., Exodus 18:4; Deuteronomy 33:7, 26, 29; Psalms 20:2; 33:20 etc.). Viewed con-textually, this word is surely a most lofty and worthy description of the difference between the man and the woman, for it is elevating her to fulfil a divine function.

The word *suitable (partner)* literally means 'an over against one' in the sense of a 'counterpart'; *corresponding to* would be a good translation. It carries the meaning of complete complementarity.

> I take [*suitable*] in its general sense, as though it were said she is a kind of counterpart, for the woman is said to be *opposite to*, or *over against*, the man, because she responds to him (Calvin, Comm., *in loc.*).

The woman is therefore to be a contrary one to the man in the sense of positively stimulating and provoking him to ever higher endeavour. The man is incomplete without the woman. He needs her partnership and she has a role to play which makes both of them complete as a team of two.

By extrapolation, the complementarity of the man and woman is carried over into non-physical relationships of everyday living. In work, community and church, men and women are incomplete without each other, whereas in a proper relationship they form an effective team.

The difference that is so clearly implied in the sexual relationship of the man to the woman is their 'face-to-faceness', for Eve was Adam's bride. Just as their side-by-sideness was expressed in their relationship to God as created in his image, so their face-to-faceness also expresses their relationship to God as created in his image. For God is not a solitary being: 'God said, "Let us make man in our likeness..."' (1:26).

The Prologue of John's Gospel expounds the God of the Genesis account of creation as a Being with relationships within himself: 'the Word was with God, and the Word was God... the One and Only, who came from the Father... God the One and Only, who is at the Father's side...'. (John 1:1, 14, 18).

Therefore, it is in both our likeness to God, made in his image *male and female,* and in our difference from him, created by him as the work of his hands, that our relationship to God lies. Both *likeness* and *difference* are needed. The biblical principle taught here is that it is only as the man and the woman face God that they can face each other in fullness of complementarity.

Is this not the error of modern extreme feminism, that it seeks to have male and female stand side by side, but not face to face? It encourages women to see men as rivals, instead of as partners. And so sexuality becomes misunderstood and distorted, for in rivalry there can never be complementarity, far less true unity. And the beautiful and glorious truth of the Genesis theology of sexuality is that male and female become one in their likeness and one in their difference, in their side-by-sideness, and in their face-to-faceness. *The man and his wife were both naked, and they felt no shame* (2:25).

Is it here that we come up against the essence of sin in any homosexual genital relationship. Whether a male-male or a female-female sexual relationship, it is bound to be based on likeness, but not on difference. So such a relationship is based not only on just a part of human sexuality, but on a seriously deficient relationship with God in creation, founded on both likeness and difference.

The order between man and woman

We come to the New Testament under-standing of the theology contained in the order of creation, in that the man was made first, and then the woman. Paul takes this to mean that the man is the *head* of the woman (1 Corinthians 11:3; Ephesians 5:23; 1 Timothy 2:13): e.g., 'the head of every man is Christ, and the head of woman is man, and the head of Christ is God' (1 Corinthians 11:3).

It is axiomatic in Pauline theology that Christ is the Son of God, and as the Son, is co-equal with the Father. The name which is above every name, that he is Lord, implies both his deity and equality with God. Nevertheless, Paul can also say that *the head of Christ is God*. So in some way, equality does not exclude headship on the one hand, nor submission to that headship on the other hand.

The Hebrew understanding of *the head* needs to be studied in detail (which is outwith the scope of this article on Genesis 1 and 2). But we can affirm that in Hebrew thought 'thinking' and 'mind' were not thought of as within the head. Rather, the head was seen as the source of life. And since Adam was created first in Genesis 2, it is not difficult to see why Paul calls him *the head*.

God is called *the head of Christ*, since the Son is eternally begotten. God's headship of Christ speaks of the eternal generation of the Son, that is, the Son eternally derives life from the Father. The Son is head of the church in that he is *the firstborn* of the resurrection, and thus the prototype of the new creation. But since God raised him from the dead, God is still his source of life.

However, the other side of the coin is undoubtedly the submission given by Christ to God as head, which submission the woman is invited to give to the man as head. There can be no doubt that the reason for the common objections raised to such submission are given in Genesis 3:16c: 'Your desire will be for your husband…' (cf. 4:7b: 'sin is crouching at your door; it desires to have you…'); here the meaning appears to be that the Fall has robbed the man-woman relationship of its perfect complementarity, and substituted in its place an uneasy rivalry.

But there is no such rivalry between Father and Son (Philippians 2:6ff. 'who, being in very nature God, did not consider equality with God something to be grasped, but made himself nothing'), and therefore Christ's submission to his Father was an expression of perfect love for the Father, as was the Father's will for the Son.

Headship in the New Testament sense, therefore, can only work harmoniously when both man and woman are in Christ, and the submission of the woman (as an equal to an equal) is lovingly offered to the man as a gift from one who is both side by side and face to face with him. More, if the woman does not freely give that submission, then the 'order between man and woman' in Christ cannot happen. By the same token, unless the man, with Christ also as his role-model, does not love the woman with a sacrificial, self-denying, self-giving love (Ephesians 5:25ff.), then neither can his headship be a harmonious constituent of the partnership.

Adam was formed first... (1 Timothy 3:13). The underlying principle in the Hebrew mind of Paul is probably that of the responsibility the first-born must assume for the family. This would be in keeping with the biblical emphasis on 'responsibility', and its almost total silence on 'rights' in this sense: the employer is told of his responsibilities towards his employee but nothing of his rights as an employer; similarly the employee is told of his responsibilities towards his employer, but nothing of his rights as an employee. So, also in the husband-wife relationship (Ephesians 5:21-33; 6:5-9).

The respect the wife is exhorted to give to her husband is therefore to one who is not just the 'source of life' in a rudimentary, physical sense, but rather to one to whom has been

17

committed the responsibility to care and provide for his family. Not that such responsibility of the husband precludes the co-operation and partnership of his wife, but that every team must have a captain, and, even though the captain is not the best player in the team, the team cannot function harmoniously unless the captain is allowed to perform the captain's role, and is fully supported in that role.

Conclusion

Genesis 1-2 give the foundation of a Biblical theology of sexuality, in the loving purpose of the Creator. The one word which could summarize that sexuality might be 'complementarity'. Genesis 3 comments theologically on the disharmony and state of rivalry between the sexes which is endemic in human society.

The good news of Jesus Christ offers the path to a new harmony which can be achieved in the relationship between the sexes, as the Spirit of God does his work, through Christ and his example. Thus there begins in men and women the divine restoration of the image of God so seriously marred through our human selfishness.

Chapter Two

Romans 1: 24, 26, 27
and the Modern Sexuality Debate

Geoffrey Grogan

This passage is crucial for the modern debate on homosexuality. In recent years, it has featured in the work of writers like John Boswell,[1] Robin Scroggs[2] and William Countryman[3] on the one hand, and Richard Hays,[4] David F. Wright[5] and Thomas Schmidt[6] on the other.

---

[1] John Boswell, *Christianity, Social Tolerance and Homosexuality*, Chicago, 1980.

[2] Robin Scroggs, *The New Testament and Homosexuality*, Philadelphia, 1983.

[3] L. William Countryman, *Dirt, Greed and Sex*, London, 1989.

[4] Richard B. Hays, 'Relations, Natural and Unnatural: A Response to John Boswell's Exegesis of Romans 1', in *The Journal of Religious Ethics*, 14 (1986), pp. 184-215.

[5] David F. Wright, 'Homosexuality: The Relevance of the Bible' in *The Evangelical Quarterly*, 61:6 (1989), pp. 291-300.

[6] Thomas E Schmidt, 'Impurity and Sin in Romans 1:26-27' (an unpublished paper—a response to Countryman). See also his treatment in *Straight and Narrow? Compassion and Clarity in the Homosexual Debate*, Leicester, IVP, 1995.

Boswell has argued that Paul is branding as sinful only homosexual acts committed by people with heterosexual orientation; Scroggs has argued that what Paul condemns is aggressive pederasty[7] and that there is no way of knowing what he would say about mutually consenting and committed homosexual relationships by people who have a natural homosexual orientation; Countryman has argued that Paul treats active homosexuality not as sin but as a form of ceremonial impurity and that he regarded such impurity as having no bearing on the conduct of Gentile Christians.

In their various ways, these three writers are united in asserting that Romans 1 cannot be used to brand such relationships today as sinful. It is well worth noting, however, that they are anything but agreed as to the way they interpret the passage. Is this significant? It might seem ungracious to suggest they are determined at all costs to evade the painful meaning of the passage, but there is surely at least a case to answer here!

Hays, Wright and Schmidt all criticize the exegesis on which these views are based, and

---

[7] Pederasty (paederasty) is the practice of having a child or an adolescent as a homosexual lover.

they contend for a basically traditional exegesis of the passage.

At the outset, we should observe the call of Richard Hays for questions of exegesis and hermeneutics to be clearly distinguished.[8] (Exegesis: 'the original meaning intended by Paul'; hermeneutics: 'the significance of what Paul says for our problems today'.) He is surely right. It is a serious error of method to approach the text immediately with modern issues in mind, reading it in their light. We need, first of all, to consider its meaning in its literary and historical setting. As Robin Scroggs says, 'Until we know what the biblical authors were against we cannot begin to reflect upon the relevance of those writings for contemporary issues.'[9] Hays criticizes Boswell for failing to follow this methodology.

The meaning of the text for Paul and his first readers

(i) Paul writes to expound the gospel as the revelation of God's righteousness. Romans 1:16-17 is widely recognised as the key programmatic text of the epistle. For instance,

---

[8] *Op. cit.,* p. 1.
[9] *Op. cit.,* p. 1.

J.C. Beker[10] holds that the theme of Romans revolves around four interrelated issues, all of which are found in these two verses. There has been much discussion of the purpose of the letter, but virtually all scholars treat this text as important in their assessment of the letter's main purpose.

If then we read the verses we are to consider in the light of 1:16-17, this will mean that the human condition as it appears here is not necessarily final, so that the gospel holds out hope to those who are caught up in sin. Its message of grace and therefore of divinely-given hope for the sinner should constantly be borne in mind.

(ii) Paul sees human history as the revelation of God's wrath in its reaction against human godlessness and unrighteousness. The positive exposition of the gospel in terms of the righteousness of God commences at Romans 3:21. Prior to this, Paul deals with the revelation of God's wrath against human godlessness and unrighteousness. It is particularly important to see that this passage is not simply about sin but about the way

[10] J.C. Becker, 'The Faithfulness of God and the Priority of Israel in Paul's Letter to the Romans' in K.P. Donfried (ed.) *The Romans Debate,* Peabody, Mass., 1991, pp. 329-32.

God's wrath is revealed against it. This makes its theme a very solemn one.

Paul views God's wrath as revealed both historically and eschatologically. The eschatological dimension of his wrath and judgment is seen in 2:1-16 and 3:5-8, the historical in 1:18-32. Paul uses the present continuous tense of *apocaluptein* ('reveal') in 1:18 and most of the verbs in the passage that follow this are in the aorist, so that he appears to be contemplating the whole of human history including its contemporary phase, without of course making reference to particular events.

So he is not writing about individual sin but rather about the disclosure of God's wrath in the whole human story. We should note that his threefold use of *paradidomi* ('give up') in verses 24, 26, 28 is consistently in the aorist, which is of course the most natural tense for historical discourse. F.F. Bruce appropriately quotes a saying of Schiller, 'The history of the world is the judgment of the world.'[11]

The historical nature of this passage is in fact in line with the historical concentration of Romans, for passages like 3:19-26, 4:1-25, 5:12-

---

[11] F.F. Bruce, writing on Romans 1:18 in *The Epistle to the Romans*, London, 1963, *ad loc.*

21, 8:18-25 and chapters 9 to 11 are all historical or historical/eschatological in form.

(iii) He sees sin as the result of God's wrath as well as its cause. The way *paradidomi* is used here shows this clearly. Verses 18-23 look like an exposition of 'godlessness' and verses 24-32 of 'unrighteousness'. It is at the start of this second section that this verb is employed for the first time. It attributes what follows to the reprobating activity of God. Humanity's wilful rebellion against the light of creation concerning the nature of God is the moral cause of this reprobating activity, so that this godlessness becomes the cause of unrighteousness.

The phrase *godlessness and unrighteousness* functions as a kind of rubric, covering all that follows to the end of the chapter. It is not easy, therefore, on contextual grounds, to agree to Countryman's reduction of terms normally understood to be ethical (and so related to sin) so that they become ceremonial (and so related to purity).

Thomas E. Schmidt has also shown the lexical basis of Countryman's argument cannot bear investigation, and that at least eight of the terms used in the key verses should be understood ethically. We cannot pursue his arguments[12] in detail here, but it is worth noting that he maintains, surely correctly, that if even one of them is ethical, this crucial part of Countryman's argument falls. His one concession to Countryman is that *plane*, at the close of verse 27, ought to be seen as a theological rather than an ethical term and translated *error* (AV, RSV) rather than *perversion* (NIV).

(iv) He views the moral exchange involved in homosexuality as an appropriate penalty for the theological exchange involved in idolatry. Paul uses *allaso* in verse 23 and its compound *metallasso* in verses 25 and 26, both normally translated 'exchange'. His use of the compound verb *metallasso* in consecutive verses, first with reference to idolatry and then to homosexuality, surely implies some parallel between the theological and moral errors. Then because he uses *paradidomi* ('give up') between the two compound verbs suggests that the second occurrence of *metallasso* in reference to homosexuality is an appropriate penalty for first which refers to idolatry.

This understanding of the passage is strengthened when we note Paul's use of *physicen* ('natural') in verses 26 and 27.

---

[12] *Op. cit.*, pp. 4-18.

Cranfield says, 'By "natural" and "contrary to nature" Paul clearly means "in accordance with the Creator's intention" and "contrary to the Creator's intention" respectively.'

The context shows a number of important linguistic parallels with the Septuagint (the Greek translation) of Genesis 1. Cranfield's further comment is therefore appropriate when he says, 'It is not impossible that Paul had some awareness of the great importance which for centuries "nature" had in Greek thought; that he was aware of its use in contemporary popular philosophy is very likely. But the decisive factor in his use of it is the biblical doctrine of creation.'[13]

Is Paul's language restricted to homosexual activity which was closely linked to idolatry and was part of pagan worship? No, for when he writes of 'the sinful desires of their hearts' (v. 24), 'shameful lusts' (v. 26), and of people being 'inflamed with lust' (v. 27) he is using pejorative language which is distinctly ethical rather than religious.

To apply this language simply to heterosexuals acting against their nature by committing homosexual acts is to commit

---

[13] Both quotations from C.E.B. Cranfield, *Romans: A Shorter Commentary*, Edinburgh, 1985, *ad loc.*

gross anachronism, for it assumes a distinction between 'natural' and 'unnatural' homosexuality which was totally foreign to all thinking, whether Jewish, Greek or Roman, at the time when Paul was writing.

Certainly, pederasty was the common form of homosexuality in Paul's day, but the wider bearing of his language becomes clear, as David Wright has pointed out, when we see that he includes female homosexual activity too.[14] This was very little recorded in Paul's world and yet he makes reference to it in parallel terms to male behaviour. Can there be any doubt that he intended to make blanket reference to homosexual activity as such as being contrary to the Creator's intention and therefore sinful?

(v) Regarding Paul's meaning in this passage, we may conclude he is here indicating that homosexual activity, both male and female, and without further distinction, is contrary to the Creator's intention, that its existence in the world is an appropriate penalty for the worship of elements of the creation instead of the Creator, and that it is therefore a manifestation of his present wrath, which will be finally revealed at the day of judgment.

---

[14] D.F. Wright, *op. cit.*, p. 295.

There is, however, hope if sinful human beings will put their faith (a penitent faith, as Romans 6:1ff. implies) in God through Christ.

Application of the passage to the current debate

If the passage refers to all homosexual activity without distinction and regards it as contrary to the Creator's intention and therefore as both a manifestation of his present wrath and subject to the final revelation of that wrath in eschatological judgment, the question of its application today is highly important.

Paul's teaching here is closely related to teaching of fundamental importance in biblical theology. If Paul is a consistent writer, with the Christian *kerygma* ('proclamation', i.e. 'what is proclaimed', 'the message') as the factor which gives integration to all he says, this kerygmatic basis of his thought is never more evident than it is in this epistle. Romans 1:16-17 is one of the clearest brief statements of that *kerygma* in his extant writings, and the letter itself is Paul's *magnum opus* on the nature and implications, both theological and ethical, of that *kerygma*.

Moreover, he is writing to a church where he has not yet laboured, and yet, at least in this section of the epistle, he apparently sees no need to argue for the position he takes, strongly suggesting that it was common to that apostolic teaching which was normative for all the churches.

In addition, his thought is grounded in the Old Testament, and not simply in the outlook of contemporary Judaism. As Hays has pointed out,[15] there may be an allusion to Leviticus 18:22 and 20:13 in Romans 1:32, but the chief Old Testament background is to be found in the basic creation theology of Genesis 1. This creation theology reappears, not only in Psalm 8, Ecclesiastes, in so-called Deutero-Isaiah and in many other parts of the Old Testament, but, even more importantly, also in the teaching, including the ethical teaching, of Jesus. It is identifiable as part of what C.H. Dodd, in *According to the Scriptures*, calls the sub-structure of the New Testament theology.

For all these reasons, it would seem impossible to hold, with George Edwards,[16] that Paul is simply giving an account of conventional Jewish attitudes towards

---

[15] *Op. cit.*, p. 206.
[16] George R. Edwards, *Gay/Lesbian Liberation: A Biblical Perspective*, New York, 1984.

Gentiles in order to set up his later rejection of Jewish self-righteousness.

It is true that the New Testament has little teaching on the homosexual issue, but teaching such as Paul gives here, which relates to such central themes of New Testament and Old Testament theology, is thereby given an importance which makes its rejection serious if we have any desire to be biblical Christians.

New Testament Christian ethics affirm Old Testament ethics. It might of course be argued that the Mosaic legislation does not necessarily apply to Christians. Paul's use of the language of Genesis 1, however, grounds his teaching in the created order. In particular, verse 23, which refers to images resembling mortal man or birds or animals or reptiles (RSV), uses Greek words all but one of which (the exception is 'mortal'), are to be found in Genesis 1:20-26. The Jews have always placed special emphasis on the relevance of the creation order and the Noachian ordinances for human life generally and this would appear to be sound and an approach with which Christians can identify.

In discussing the Mosaic legislation, Paul argues from the temporal priority of the

Abrahamic covenant (Galatians 3:15-18). Even more significantly, in an ethical discussion, Jesus himself argued from the temporal priority of the teaching of Genesis 2 about marriage (Matthew 19:8-9). Moreover, family relationships, which in Scripture go right back to early Genesis, are of central importance in New Testament ethical teaching.

In the creation narratives, fundamental issues concerning the nature of God, of human beings and of their relationship to each other are in view, and this material forms the basic framework for all that the Bible writers say about that relationship both in terms of divine judgment and of divine redemption.

We cannot reckon any form of homosexual behaviour to be exempt from the strictures of this passage. This follows from Paul's grounding of his thought in the created order. In fact, he sees human nature to be deeply affected by sin, and, if there is now such a thing as 'natural homosexuality', there can be little doubt that he would regard this as itself part of the global consequences of humanity's departure from God. As Hays points out, 'Paul's condemnation of homosexual activity does not rest on an assumption that it is freely chosen; indeed it is precisely characteristic of

31

Paul to regard "sin" as a condition of human existence, a condition which robs us of free volition and drives us to disobedient actions which, though involuntary, are nonetheless culpable (see especially Romans 7:13-25). That is what it means to live "in the flesh" in a fallen creation.'[17]

However, there are no biblical grounds for regarding homosexuality as 'the sin of sins', and the sensitive Christian, recognizing his or her own sinfulness, will feel a deep pastoral concern for the person struggling with homosexuality and the special problems that person faces, while, in faithfulness to Scripture, treating all homosexual genital activity as contrary to God's creative intention and therefore as sinful.

As Paul's thought is grounded in the creation order, we cannot reckon any form of homosexual behaviour exempt from the strictures of this passage. Also, however, the Christian both believes from Scripture and knows in personal experience the grace of God to sinners and so can bring a wonderful message of hope to the penitent.

---

[17] *Op. cit.*, p. 209.

Chapter Three

Some Issues Raised by the Homosexuality Debate

David F. Wright

Of one thing we may be sure: challenging issues about sexual relationships other than heterosexual marriage will not go away, whatever the General Assembly of the Church of Scotland or any church body decides. The reason for this is simple—that the acceptance of such relationships is widespread in our society, and in particular has deep roots in influential areas of British culture, both popular and more sophisticated.

Another reason is more worrying: some of the opinion-formers within the mainstream churches seem to view these developments almost as bearers of fresh wisdom from God. The social realities of sexual behaviour are no longer, it seems, to be evaluated in the light of God's once-for-all self-revelation in Christ; they may even be held to constitute norms which the churches ignore at their peril. As a recent Archbishop of York once put it, unless the Church of England changes its mind on divorce, it will lose touch with the people—as though the latter is more to be feared than departing from what the Church believes to be the mind of God. Such an attitude informs many a revisionist approach to these questions, even if it is not expressed in such naked terms.

We may expect, therefore, that Christians who see no reason to abandon traditional teaching grounded in Scripture will increasingly find themselves swimming against the tide. The Christian lifestyle will become more and more counter-cultural, and because of the growing acceptance, in sectors of mixed denominations, of sub-Christian patterns of behaviour (as they have hitherto been universally regarded), internal church divisions are likely to widen. The cohesiveness of a body like the Church of Scotland will surely be tested as never before —if (which God forbid) it tolerates elders living together outside marriage or practicing homosexuals pairing off in the manse.

Pastors and teachers who are sensitive to the signs of the times will already be equipping their congregations, especially at the younger end, to live against the stream. I sometimes wonder if ministers are direct or explicit enough in their teaching on sexual morality. A proper modesty may have its place, but sometimes too much is taken for granted. Why is it that from time to time students (even Christian students) turn up in university never having heard that sex outside marriage is wrong? It is an odd situation if every other means of communication that influences our lives calls a spade a spade apart from the pulpit.

Moreover, we have to be ready with more than straight affirmation. The arguments of the revisionists must be shown to be wanting. What follows will attempt to provide some guidance for this task.

Relationships: values versus form?

It is often said that what matters is not the structure of a relationship, but the qualities that inform it. What gives it integrity are virtues like trust, openness, commitment and acceptance, irrespective of whether it conforms to God's design. Much better, so it is claimed, a partnership that displays these values, whether heterosexual or homosexual, than a loveless, shrivelled marriage. As countless pop songs put it, love is all you need —scarcely different from the 'new morality' of a generation ago (John Robinson, Harry

Williams *et al.*) which opposed love to law and first taught Christians that sex outside marriage might, with love, be OK. (What a fearful responsibility that 'new morality' generation bears for our present disorders!

If we take our bearings from Scripture, this is a false choice. Divinely ordered relationships and God-given qualities belong together. The fact that some marriages go sour is no warrant for dispensing with marriage. There is no basis in Scripture for believing that love and other Christian qualities justify or hallow an improper relationship. It is undeniable that cohabiting couples may show deep and selfless affection for each other, and that a gay partnership may be marked by enviable mutual care. (We have no interest in rubbishing all such relationships as fired by selfish gratification.) But they fall short in varying degrees of God's plan for one-to-one relationships in which alone is sexual fulfilment to be found. Honour among thieves may be truly admirable, but it does not sanction thieving.

Starting at the beginning: the heterosexual norm

There are few things as fundamental in the biblical revelation as the divine ordering of heterosexual monogamy. It is found throughout Scripture—for example, in two of the Ten Commandments, in the teaching of Jesus, where it is reaffirmed and its implications deepened, and in Ephesians as an image of the love between Christ and his church. To excise or override this foundation is to do deep structural damage to the teaching of Scripture. And if it is objected that Jesus, the perfect human being, was not married, that very fact marked him out as destined for a highly exceptional calling among his contemporaries.

We must refuse to let go of this starting point. Too many discussion documents from churches in recent years have begun elsewhere—with a general or common sexuality celebrated as God's gift. Only later do they go on to consider the proper expressions of this sexuality. But the Bible knows nothing of an undifferentiated or abstract sexuality, which may be exercised in different ways. From start to finish it presents heterosexuality—men created as sexual beings for sexual matching with women, and women likewise for men. To abandon this basis (which is embodied in the differing anatomies of male and female) is to set off on the wrong foot at the outset.

So the biblical case for disapproving of homosexual conduct does not rest on a few contested texts, but on a widely pervasive feature of the revealed wisdom of God for human life. Yet the explicit New Testament references (Romans 1:26-27, 1 Corinthians 6:9) carry a heavier punch than revisionists allow. (See my Cutting Edge series booklet *The Christian Faith and Homosexuality*, and more fully my article in *Evangelical Quarterly* 61, 1989, pp. 291-300, 'Homosexuality: the Relevance of the Bible'. The best book on the whole issue is Thomas E. Schmidt, *Straight and Narrow? Compassion and Clarity in the Homosexuality Debate*, from IVP.)

Not forgetting the Fall

Against this backcloth of God's creative blueprint, the many distortions of sexual disposition and behaviour in human society have to be understood in terms of the fallenness of all humankind. In the case of homosexuality, this applies to orientation as well as to behaviour, and this will not change if or when a genetic explanation for the homosexual condition is discovered.

There is no mileage in denying or resisting the identification of genetic factors as wholly or partly responsible for homosexual tendencies. To do otherwise would be to take refuge in something like God-of-the-gaps theology in reverse, as though only in the gaps in current genetic science could one discern the effects of the Fall.

It is no new challenge for biblical Christians to regard deeply ingrained inclinations or orientations in men and women, whether genetically caused or not, as part of the detritus of the fallenness of the race. In this respect, as in others, homosexuality must not be isolated either from the reach of basic Christian beliefs or from other conditions, such as alcoholism, kleptomania or paedophilia.

Loving the sinner, hating the sin

This sounds glib and facile, and is often resented by gay lobbyists as insulting. Yet it is surely, as a general phrase, no more—and no less!—than what the core message of Christianity is all about. If the mission of Jesus, and the reason why the incarnate Son was given this human name, was to save us from our sins, then not only the distinction between sinners and their sins, but also the separation of one from the other, lie at the heart of things. Again, this approach to homosexuality sets it in the context of the gospel which encompasses all sorts and conditions of men and women. I emphasize this point in the face of denials, implicit or explicit, that homosexuals need, or can benefit from, the central message of the Christian gospel, which summons us all—or rather, only sinners, not the righteous!—to faith and repentance.

Human identity—in creation and in Christ

One reason why revisionists resent 'love the sinner, hate the sin' is that they treat homosexuality as constitutive of a person's identity. Talk of sundering a man or woman from this or her homosexuality is thus felt as a threat to their essential being. What they demand is acceptance specifically as gay or lesbian.

This sense of hurt calls for a sensitive response. It may well be the case that when we talk about homosexuality in any public gathering, one or more of those listening will feel that their whole being is under challenge. We need to be aware of this possibility, without accepting the assumptions and instincts it represents. It may be understandable, in a society so preoccupied with heterosexual sexual fulfilment as ours appears to be, why persons of different sexual disposition should perceive their identity so much in terms of this difference.

But it is surely far healthier to insist that our worth as human beings consists in our being created in God's image and recreated in Christ. No higher value can be placed on a man or woman than this. It is a particularly worrying feature of the gay and lesbian Christian movement that it seeks recognition of homosexuals precisely in terms of their homosexuality, instead of as creatures of God, sinful like all of us but capable of being remade in Christ. Others do not rest their personal identity in their heterosexuality!

Acceptance and non-acceptance

The domination of late-twentieth-century liberal Christianity by an almost antinomian inclusivism is reflected in the way 'acceptance' has ousted 'forgiveness'. Forgiveness recognizes, and acceptance often implicitly denies, the need for repentance. Christ accepts us as sinners, but accepts us in forgiveness, not in mere recognition that we are who we are. And where there is room for forgiveness (and there is no acceptance by God without it), there is room for hearts and lives to be changed. Jesus refused to condemn the adulteress to the punishment Jewish law required, but his acceptance of her accompanied a sharp summons to abandon her adultery. Much the same can be said of the use of 'affirm' (except that grammatically it is much odder to say 'the gospel affirms me'!)

Evangelical churches above all others should be places where the good news of a forgiving and welcoming God is heard in unmistakable tones by sinners of all kinds —including the notorious offenders of the Gospels. But there is no hint in the Gospels that Jesus approved or tolerated prostitutes continuing to ply their trade or tax-gatherers continuing to fleece taxpayers. The Scottish Reformed tradition has probably erred in the direction of legalism, but this is no excuse for swinging to the other extreme of cheap grace that makes no moral demands and expects no moral renewal.

Reading the Bible whole: or, against separating what God has joined together

The revisionist liberalism that is now ready to accept non-marital heterosexual and same-sex relationships often seems a throwback to the Jesus-only liberalism of an earlier era. The Old Testament and Paul are largely pensioned off as incurably patriarchal, in an exclusive appeal to the Jesus of the Gospels. Yet even this is not free from selectivity—citing John 8:11a but omitting John 8:11b. A church in the Reformed tradition should be the last to excise the Old Testament from the Bible as did Marcion,[1] if it is faithful to its true genius.

It is difficult to take seriously as an argument in favour of accepting homosexual behaviour that Jesus said nothing about it. If this is indeed the case, it would not be surprising. Jesus said nothing about a great many topics that were not live issues in Palestine in his day—like social security schemes, democracy and votes for all, and equal pay for women (and even about many that presumably were, like nationalism, housing the homeless, disarmament and the care of the terminally ill). And it is agreed that homosexuality became an issue for the Jews only when they spread into the Hellenistic world (just as earlier it had been an issue for Israel only when encountered among its Canaanite neighbours).

This argument from the silence of Jesus is a kind of negative proof texting—and reflects a naively unhistorical treatment of the Gospels.

---

[1] A 2nd century 'would-be' church reformer who was excommunicated in AD144 for his Gnostic heresies.

As such, it is another instance of the arbitrary selectivity that the revisionist case relies on throughout: it severely restricts the relevance of the Old Testament and most of the New Testament, apart from the Gospels, on the grounds of their historical relativism (they reflect the social and cultural worlds in which they originated), but asks questions of the Gospels in a totally non-historical fashion. If any of the Bible is historically conditioned, all of it is. There is no core-gospel (not even 'God is love') which comes to us except in a particular vocabulary (first-century Greek in this case), from a particular context (that of 1 John, its author and recipients). 'God is love' is true in a biblical sense, i.e. as biblically warranted, only when 'God' and 'love' are given their first-century contextualized meanings—not as any modern might care to conceive of God and love!

Note well: the sound response to 'But that's all patriarchalism!' is not to try to carve out some reserved territory free of this plague, but to insist that there is no self-revelation of God except that given under such socio-cultural limitations. Jesus was not incarnate except as a Jew in first-century Palestine, nor crucified except 'under Pontius Pilate', and the New Testament comes to us only in Hellenistic

44

Greek. We either accept—and glory in!—the scandal of particularity, or set about creating our own religion in embarrassment at the once-for-all givenness of historic Christianity.

So the debate about homosexuality turns out to encapsulate a number of the critical issues in the battle to hold on to a Christianity that is recognizably the faith of our mothers and fathers. The alternative is a faith that is made in our own image, and made anew in every generation. But of a faith in which we see the reflection, narcissistically, of our contemporary society's values and aspirations, one thing is sure—it cannot save contemporary society. A gospel adjusted to accommodate even the best of today's insights and wisdom will be so different a gospel that it will not even be (in Paul's words) 'another gospel' at all (see Galatians 1:6-7).

Chapter Four

A Pastoral Perspective on the Problems of our Fallen Sexuality

William Still[1]

Sexuality is an inherent part of human nature with its own unique drive in mature and maturing adults. It is astonishing, therefore, that its legitimate sphere, as far as the Bible is concerned, is laid down as only within the confines of marriage—the joining of man and woman together in sexual union. This virtually excludes overt sexual experience as a relevant, moral subject for the celibate.

Freud and others have tried to show that sex increases human happiness, but an article in *The Times* in January 1993[2] said simply that sex results in great unhappiness as people vainly try to live up to the ideal. And when sex doesn't bring joy and pleasure, says Liz

---

[1] The late William Still, minister in Gilcomston South Church, Aberdeen, for 56 years, remained single all his life.

[2] Liz Hodgkinson, 'Body and Mind: Lightness of Being Celibate', in *The Times*, Tuesday 19 January, 1993.

Hodgkinson in this article, we can start to blame and even hate the partner—or ourselves. She says:

> Many people discover that their physical health improves during a time of voluntary celibacy. This is because sex brings into play a large amount of stress hormones, which can eventually lead to stress-related diseases. Although a life of celibacy is popularly imagined to be one of misery, deprivation and continual frustration and repression, it can be the very opposite, and provide a wonderful opportunity to get to know yourself, understand who you are and what is your real purpose in life. It can also allow to develop hitherto undiscovered talents. A period of voluntary celibacy can give space and time to become autonomous and self-sufficient. It can bestow a powerful feeling of liberation and lightness. It means you can truly reclaim yourself, and become free from the sexual demands of your own body and also the sexual desires of other people, which you may not always feel like accommodating.

Well, are you wondering if you are reading alright? It's a change, you must agree, from most that we hear, read or see about sex these days. Most evocative, if not provocative enough for a celibate (like myself) to gloat over it shockingly! Nonetheless, sex is undoubtedly a dominating factor in human life, directly and indirectly; it relates to, and affects, practically every sphere of adult life, so much so that any tampering with its potential in childhood is almost bound to have a deleterious effect upon growing children, and may injure the whole of their subsequent adult life.

The problems are legion

One is obliged to ask, 'How are we to regard sexuality in its general effect on human life?' Some might suggest the answer is marriage. But even within marriage, its problems are legion, as every pastor will testify.

For example, withholding conjugal rights, for whatever reason—whether incompatibility, or because of undue sexual demands—can lead to such a temptation to the other spouse towards unlawful extramarital relations as to be a frequent source of sexual immorality. Therefore, to seek for sexual, as well as spiritual, moral, intellectual, and emotional, compatibility is a high responsibility in a world in which there is such diversity of human nature.

In a fallen world, it is far from surprising that so many individuals either never find sexual harmony, or having found it, regard it so lightly that the sinful questing of their personality looks for extramarital sexual experience. The result is inevitably the dis-ordering of at least three lives, and often many more, especially where offspring are involved.

Marriage breakdown

The possibilities of sexual incompatibility or misalliance are so infinite that it would seem a miracle that any, or certainly many, should find complete harmony in marriage; hence sexual immorality must be one of the greatest moral problems known to man. The marvel is that so many do find sexual harmony and produce children, and that then these children themselves in turn find sexual compatibility within the lawful canons of biblical morality. Our concern in this article is with those who don't!

Even amongst professing Christians, advoc-ates of Christianity and the 'professionally religious', marriage breakdowns occur too frequently. If for the majority of souls there is a marital partner to be found within their normal daily orbit—and bear in mind that many are often obliged to make do with the best available—this surely calls for nothing less than divine guidance from him who knows all.

Divine canons

In the midst of the infinite variety of the problems of sexual immorality, the canons of biblical guidance and restraint are such that, where they are acknowledged and observed, they limit the injury that can be inflicted on the human personality. But that requires a high degree of both morality and spirituality.

To commit oneself wholly to Christ, for him to govern the totality of one's life, will mean that his help will be enlisted in, at least, damage limitation. A very great deal can be done in that sphere where the presence, help and comfort of the Lord is sought to achieve containment of one's sexual desires within the necessary restraints which need to govern distressing experiences of non-satisfaction.

It is in such situations that an involvement and encounter with the living Christ can make all the difference between the immoral ruin of a life which finds itself the victim of unhappy, unfulfilled sexual experience, or a life which finds approximate fulfillment and satisfaction within the constraints of happy sexual experience. A person who (for whatever reason) has been divorced, or bereaved of a spouse, is for a season (at least), deprived of sexual fulfillment. He or she needs special grace, as well as the prayers of sympathetic Christian friends, to prove the value of restraint under biblical laws. And to find, perhaps temporarily, a lifestyle in which the sexual drive finds other than sexual outlets and expressions.

Spiritual and moral help

Of course, all who have not found sexual compatibility in marriage need spiritual and moral help. The frustration of sexual desire is a major experience in any life, and there is no end to the forms of counsel which could be offered to persons in such situations. Certainly those who have known sexual satisfaction to some extent and then for some reason have been deprived of it, need very special help. They suffer such a profound loss that nothing but the understanding of a loving heavenly Father and his incarnate Son can assuage. The solution may be another lawful sexual union. It may also be commitment to a life of self-denial in which the good Lord is almost bound to provide some other direction for a now frustrated and unfulfilled urge.

When one thinks of the infinite possibilities of sexual maladjustment, it is of all things the possibility of friendship with the Lord Jesus which is by far the greatest factor in finding solutions to such problems. Indeed, in these circumstances there can be few as comforting words as those which say, 'Like as a father pities his children, so the Lord pities them that fear him. For he knows our frame; he remembers that we are dust.'

It can only be the enemy of souls who keeps Christian people from giving wholehearted attention to such a comforting promise. As in so much of the Christian life, peace and satisfaction are found in keeping the enemy and his nefarious tricks at bay to permit us to enjoy the Lord and his satisfactions, whatever other satisfactions may be withheld from us.

Containment and redirection

That being the case, there is a sexuality which finds its exercise and fulfilment in what may be called redirection, that is, not in physical sexual satisfaction as such. It must be said that, contrary to what some carnal spirits would allege, sexual containment is far from injurious to life, but can be a blessing in disguise, because its drive may be redirected towards other, higher satisfactions. The chiefest of those is the affection which should accompany all sexual experience, but which can be expressed ad infinitum where there is no possibility of physical sexual experience, yet where that affectionate regard which is the essence of good sexual relations can be expressed with absolutely no sexual arousal at all.

This is not to say that sexual feeling ceases to exist. Far from it. But it must be admitted that it thereafter takes a considerably lesser place in one's reckoning than formerly. Is this not a great advantage, providing at least a partial solution to sexual frustration? There is this other way! An alternative indeed, which *The Times* article, quoted above, discussed, a way which the stormy sexual passions of the carnally demanding souls simply have not found.

And surely this is the way we must approach the problems of all who are sexually deprived, whatever their sexual problems may be.

Where that deprivation is within the marriage bond on account of the sinful withholding of lawful marital rights by one spouse from the other, study 1 Corinthians 7:3-7 to see what God says about mutual obligations. The limitation prescribed by the seventh commandment with regard to adultery, and the warnings in the pastoral epistles with regard to continence within the marriage bond (1 Timothy 2:2-12; 5:9; Titus 1:6), indicate that this frustration needs to be borne with continence within the realms of grace. Within those realms there are always such divine compensations as the goodness of God in his grace may be pleased to provide (e.g., 1 Samuel 1:8).

Fortunately, the Scriptures as indicated above are wonderfully explicit about problems within the marriage bond. Outside the marriage bond, however, it must be admitted that there is less help. Most of it is of a negative nature, which again is natural because outside the bonds of marriage the physical sexual urge clearly has no legitimate area of expression. The highest which is offered is containment, or redirection towards some other legitimate area of satisfaction and of affectionate service of others.

Perhaps the celibate lives of the hetero-sexual, bisexual or homosexual individuals in a Christian and biblical context are basically not so very different from each other. Some kind of subliminal continence is surely the worthy goal, along with that patience which divine grace may afford, which looks to the Lord for any further relationships which might offer legitimate satisfactions.

The possibility of change

What might such further relationships be? For the heterosexual (and for the bisexual who with growing maturity may tend to lean toward the heterosexual side), there is always the possibility that the good Lord will provide a marriage partner.

For the homosexual and bisexual who on maturing find that there is still a leaning toward the homosexual side, the matter is not so easily solved. Indeed, let it never be thought that it is beyond the powers of the Almighty, by whatever means, to correct a preponderantly homosexual urge. Because such an urge can be, and often is, exceedingly deep-seated, it will take a work of singular grace and power to dismantle and demolish the sexual feelings of years to replace them with heterosexual feelings.

A loving Father

Let it therefore now be stated, that, since we are evidently in realms of often excruciating personal spiritual and emotional agonies, it is imperative the sufferer seeks the constant comforting guidance of a loving heavenly Father. Nothing less can keep a person with a seemingly innate homosexual urge from seeking those opportunities for illegitimate

55

satisfactions of which in our modern, godless society there are too many.

Hope is said to spring eternal in the human breast. It is natural for those disorientated sexually to long for sexual satisfaction. When with maturer years neither a legitimate solution to the problem, nor a radical or miracle cure of homosexual feelings has been found, it may be necessary to conclude that it is the good Lord's will that life should be lived within that deprivation. Those faced with that prospect need to know clearly that grace will be given to bear the prohibition, lawfully and bravely, and that in God's kindness he will be pleased to provide some sort of alternative subliminal satisfaction. There are endless legitimate affectionate outlets of a caring kind for those deprived of sexual gratification, although those involved may well feel that even at best these are poor alternatives to that which is biblically forbidden.

Biblical prohibitions challenged

That the Scriptures are against homosexual practice there can be no doubt, and the conviction that this is true and right simply grows with every futile attempt made to reinterpret biblical statements in both

Testaments to allow such practice. The growing trend of such reinterpretation seen in the work of men such as John Boswell, Robin Scroggs and William Countryman,[3] has had its effect on some within Scotland—witness the Church of Scotland's Panel on Doctrine Report to the 1994 General Assembly.

Pastoral counselling

The most important thing to do with anyone who is to any extent torn between natural and unnatural sexual desire is to try to help them discourage the unnatural, and chastely to increase and normalise whatever heterosexual inclinations they may have. That can take years! That is why we should never brand anyone irrevocably homosexual under a certain age. We must give ample time under guidance to see whether with increasing maturity and the pursuance of natural sexual feelings they may be able to right themselves, or at least mortify the perverse element, if not extirpate it altogether.

A most encouraging fact is the number of men who, having passed through a seemingly homosexual stage, have emerged into hetero-

---

[3] *Submission on Human Sexuality*, Forum Paper, pub. Rutherford House, 1993. See also footnotes on p. 15.

sexuality sufficiently to contemplate marriage, and in marriage and family life have found a solution to their problem enough to make life tolerable and stable. It needs to be said, however, that homosexual feelings may still arise, especially in susceptible encounters. But by grace these experiences may be successfully mortified, so that normal married and family life goes on, whether the spouse knows about the other's problem or not. (Some women are able to cope with the knowledge of their husbands' tendencies, whereas some can hardly bear to know about them at all. Of course, abhorrence can stem from an unrealistic and unwisely idealistic attitude towards the hazards of human life. We are all sinners, and pharisaical sinners are surely the worst. See what Jesus has to say about that!)

On the other hand, some have precipitately entered into marriage in the hope that their problem of disoriented sexuality would thereby be solved, and many pastors have seen how hopeless that can be. It all depends on the degree of bias towards one sex or the other. This situation generally needs to be pastorally monitored over a period of months and even years, to see where the bias eventually may lean. If it continues increasingly to be on the homosexual side, the worst possible advice would be to marry! That has ruined many lives and broken the hearts of many men and women.

The confirmed homosexual

Let us now consider the confirmed homosexual. We must return to the basic fact that God hates what is unnatural, and nothing can make him change his mind about the abuse of the natural functions he has ordained for men and women, as for his other creatures. That is why what is called 'unisex' is quite unacceptable for Christians. The desire of women to look and behave like men, and of men to dress and develop female characteristics is contrary to creation and ought to be firmly rejected by Christian people.

This must be where we start, whoever may be hurt. But I want to appeal for a new degree of understanding. I have in view those who, through no fault of their own, are afflicted with perverse desires, and may be cruelly hounded to the point of suicide by a misguided use of the name of God and Christ. On their behalf, one must register a protest and complete condemnation of a judgmentalism which utterly ignores the infinite understanding of the holy Jesus, who, although he never excuses sin but must ever condemn it, always loves the sinner. 'Neither do I condemn you; go, and sin no more', shows the perfect balance of Christ's attitude towards all sin, but with particular reference to sexual sin.

We must distinguish between the deliberate perversity of heterosexual sinners in experimenting with homosexuality purely for 'kicks', and the sins of those who grow up with, or are seduced into homosexual inclinations and acts which then become more natural to them that the natural. Such unnatural sins, whether committed by heterosexual experimenters, or by those hooked on homosexuality, can never be excused or exonerated, nor used to overturn the biblical stance (as some are increasingly seeking to do).[4]

Christian compassion

In the interests of the compassion of Jesus Christ, there needs to be a far greater degree of understanding of why people do these things, however rightly disapproving we must be of their acts. Jesus' understanding of the woman of Samaria, the woman taken in adultery and Zacchaeus (a very different

---

[4] See Chapter 8 by Dr Trevor Stammers.

case), shows us how sad it is that in biblical, Christian, and evangelical circles there can be so much harsh, cruel and ruthless dismissal of problem people. Too often, not the slightest attempt is made to understand why they behave as they do, or to bring them to our blessed Lord's touchstone, 'Neither do I condemn you; go and sin no more'.

Our concern here is for those who for whatever reason and at whatever stage in their development have become so completely warped and twisted that to them the natural has become unnatural and the unnatural natural. It is ours to help them see that this is the work of the devil in their lives. Just as some are born with spina bifida or with other physical malformations, there are those who are either born with, or quickly acquire and develop, unnatural tendencies to the exclusion of the natural. This leads to their revulsion against what is natural. Short of a miraculous transformation by grace, they need to be helped to accept their 'thorn in the flesh', as Paul did, as a cross to be accepted for Christ's sake and used for his glory. Some of the most gifted people in the world in various realms have owed their God-used gift to the drive of sexual abnormality which has been accepted as an affliction (permitted by God,

61

though obviously attributable to fallen human nature), to be to a degree sublimated, transformed and used to the glory of God.

Godly sublimation

I have known those who were faced with extreme temptation to 'unnatural sin' who so resolutely refused to succumb to what fatally attracted them but which they knew was wrong, that I was astonished. But on reflection, I knew why their aesthetic, pastoral, and preaching gifts were signally used of God. That very drive which could have ruined them was used, when transmogrified into an instrument of God, as the means of saving and blessing many.

But let me emphasize again, that all such godly sublimation of seemingly innate sexual abnormality must be accepted and given over to God for death and transformation. This can only be done when the tendency has been recognized as a fault and flaw and not as another kind of normality! It is therefore to be mortified with a view to seeing how the Lord will re-channel its drive, if intractable, towards something to be used by God. It could then become as beautiful as the fruit of those to whom the gift of natural union is given.

Not only in the realms of artistic endeavour, but in those of loving relationships, especially in the befriending and helping of needy souls, God has used people who endure agonizingly painful deviant tendencies, but who have given their maladjustment to him for transformation. This is true of far more than many who are rigidly moralistic in the Christian world would believe! Some people hold up their hands in holy horror at even hearing that so and so has such a problem. But if they knew how sympathetic the Lord is to the affliction, and how he stands ready to use it when it is given to him, they might be shocked out of their self-righteousness.

Jesus is far more daring in what he does and whom he employs than many exceedingly pious souls dare to believe. Perhaps that's why hypocrites don't like to get too near him. He's a shocker!

The cost
But the cost to such suffering souls! Who can compute it? What the so-called incurable homosexual soul endures in loneliness and unfulfilled longing is something which long experience of sharing with such people has taught me to be nothing less than an excruciating agony. If there is one thing such a

63

person needs above all, it is counsel on two fronts: first, that affliction with an unnatural propensity, which can only come from Satan —by whatever means is beside the point— has to be accepted; and, second, like Paul's 'thorn in the flesh', it has to be given over to God for him to transform. This can be done through grace when it is sublimated into something beautiful and wonderfully useful to him. In short, what pastors must do is to face the biblical truth about such tendencies and then, accepting that if there is to be no cure, some are afflicted with warps and twists and seek God's help to find for them a true sublimation and outlet which is approved and blessed by God.

At the same time we ought to see to it that we make the sacrificial lot of these souls as comfortable as possible. Perhaps frustrated Christian counsellors should find it in their hearts to pray that it might be in the divine will for such people to find someone with whom a friendship can be formed and a level of association maintained which helps in bearing each other's burden in Christ, according to Christ's rules of purity.

Chapter Five

One Homosexual's View

There are not insignificant numbers of us in the church who have a homosexual orientation and, at the same time, are anxious to keep faith with God and to maintain biblical integrity by refusing to give physical expression to our same-sex preferences, however difficult it may be at times. We accept the message of holy Scripture in its condemnation of all homosexual acts as wrong and against God's revealed will, although such views may go against the grain of much secular thought and practice and leave us open to charges of obscurantism along with the verbal attacks of gay activists.

We reject the modern Kinsey with his crude findings that 'everyone is doing it', thereby sanctioning homosexuality as a normal alternative lifestyle, as well as the ancient Socrates arguing that homosexuality is a superior form of human love because it unites 'the love of a beautiful body with the love of a beautiful soul'. We challenge the wisdom of any of our contemporaries—however well-meaning—who advocate or endorse what is described as faithful and permanent homosexual love between Christians. Such partnerships are alien to the whole tenor of the Bible where there is neither commendation nor instructions for same-sex relationships. We have taken to heart the truth of God's Word in passages such as 1 Corinthians 6:9-10 and 1 Timothy 1:10 in its prohibition of active homosexual encounters of all kinds. As Christian believers, we honestly seek to interpret our predilection in the light of Scripture rather than interpret Scripture in the light of our predilection.

The possibility of radical change

In such an attitude of mind we approach Paul's epistle to the Corinthians, for example, acknowledging that while he does certainly classify homosexual acts as sinful he does not disdainfully single out homosexuals as worse sinners than the others mentioned. Rather than making a special sin out of homosexuality, he simply places it in the same category as drunkenness, theft and fornication. In this, God demonstrates his total impartiality toward all persons in every age. In 1 Corinthians 6:11 a pivotal statement is made: 'And such were some of you.'

Evidently, radical change has taken place and is plain for all to see. Whether living in circa AD 55 or AD 2006, we homosexuals, who have repented and believed the Good News, have abandoned our futile, godless way of life. What's more, the miraculous has happened: we are 'in Christ' and having that status we are new creatures: 'the old has gone, the new has come!' (2 Corinthians 5:17). Something of the life of God has entered us, carrying with it far-reaching implications, not least in how we perceive and cope with our particular sexual tendency, and in how we relate to those in a similar situation.

The last advice we want to hear

We suggest that in all deliberations involving the homosexual question, one important fact should be borne in mind: certain brothers and sisters now seeking to walk in that newness of life, and experiencing true freedom for the first time, have been rescued from backgrounds of appalling homosexual degradation and very likely premature deaths. Some of them will undoubtedly carry deep psychological scars for a long time to come. Because of that, it causes many of us profound distress and hurt to witness the extraordinary spectacle of spiritual leaders charged with feeding or ruling the flock of God apparently encouraging same-sex practices, however sophisticated and refined those leaders may appear to be. The last advice any of us redeemed homosexuals need to hear in our daily battles is that, in certain circumstances, the deeds that are 'natural' to us are permissible after all!

It must also be recognized that at the other extreme of experience, there are those—often younger Christians—who have a same-sex bias and thus far have led exemplary lives and wish to continue to do so despite pressures to the contrary. Surely any pastoral counsel given to them must be aimed at lovingly strengthening their resolve rather than undermining it by suggesting that a genital homosexual relationship can ever be God-given and God-sustained. In this delicate area, there is a real danger that 'little ones' who believe in Jesus are caused to sin.

Clearly, for all of us with homosexual leanings who follow Christ, and whatever our biographies, God has not left us to our own devices. In this love and compassion, he has freely and extravagantly given us the means to live as he intended in his flawless wisdom. He has sent the Holy Spirit to dwell in our hearts by faith bringing strength, comfort, victory, renewal and that unique fellowship for which we were created and purchased by our Lord's shed blood. Well can we gratefully say with Peter, 'his divine power has given us everything we need for life and godliness' (2 Peter 1:3).

Chapter Six

Singleness

David C. Searle

For centuries, singleness in western culture was regarded as an honourable state. But with the recent dramatic rise in sexual awareness through advertising and the growth of eroticism in the media, singleness has come to be regarded as an unfulfilled condition. The result of this has been increased pressure on single young people to enter into sexual relationships; unless they do—so the hype goes—they are missing out on all the excitement and fun of life. Those involved in pastoral ministry are aware that all too often marriage has been entered into inadvisedly, sometimes because singleness has come to be regarded as highly undesirable.

The other side of the 'singleness coin' is that while the churches are making some attempt to prepare couples for marriage, and also offer counselling to those whose marriages are in difficulties, little or nothing is done to help those who are single to cope with problems they may face.

Does the Bible say anything about singleness?

Although the Bible begins with the command to the man and woman to be fruitful (have children), it is clear that certain people in the Old Testament were (honourably) unmarried. We know, for example, that Jeremiah was unmarried (Jeremiah 16:2), and it may well be that Elijah was also unmarried. John the Baptist was most definitely unmarried, and Paul considered singleness necessary for him to be a missionary. Philip the Evangelist had four daughters in the unmarried category who were well known for their spiritual gifts (Acts 21:8).

However, the outstanding example of a single person in the Bible is the Lord Jesus himself. No one can accuse him of leading an unfulfilled life, even though he was unmarried. Consider briefly a comment Jesus made on the unmarried state:

> For some are eunuchs because they were
> born that way; others were made that way
> by men; and others have renounced
> marriage because of the kingdom of heaven.
> The one who can accept this should accept it
> (Matthew 19:12).

Calvin, the great reformer, made this comment on Jesus' words:

> That it is not open to all to choose which
> state they please, Christ proves from the fact
> that continence [singleness] is a special gift.
> For when he says that only those are capable
> of it to whom it is given, he plainly means
> that it is not given to all.

Calvin is saying that singleness is to be regarded as a gift of God, just as much as marriage is also a gift of God. That is the force of Jesus' words in Matthew 19:11, 'those to whom it has been given'. There can be little doubt this is how we should understand what Jesus is saying.

There are three categories of single people, according to Jesus. First, there are those who were born without the physical ability to consummate a sexual marriage relationship. Second, there are those who are single through circumstances: they would like to have been married, but the right person just never came their way. Or perhaps for reasons outside their own control, such as early sexual abuse or deep hurt caused by the break-up of their own parents' marriage, these single people have themselves never been able to face marriage. Third, there are those who have renounced marriage for the sake of the kingdom of God. Our Lord is perhaps the best example of this third category, though the church's history furnishes us with countless other examples.

The first Adam was commanded to marry and have children. But he is not our example. The second Adam (Christ) who is our example chose to be single so that he could fulfil his Father's will. Perhaps that means Christian people can make a choice because of their Lord, and be single with highest honour in order to serve God more effectively.

The situation Christians faced in New Testament times is very similar to the situation we face in society today. There was then and is now widespread promiscuity and sexual license. While Paul defends the honour of marriage as divinely given to humankind, he makes it clear that sexual relationships should be confined to the marriage bond, and he also urges that singleness is a most honourable state (see 1 Corinthians 7).

In the New Testament, then, single persons are welcomed as full participants in the work of the Lord.[1] Their single status even offers pragmatic advantages for such service. But neither the single option nor a commitment to lifelong celibacy are ever set forth as the higher road to spirituality for believers.

Living as a single

We have seen that Jeremiah, Elijah, John the Baptist, Paul and the daughters of Philip, as well as Jesus himself, could live fulfilled lives as single people. Ought it not, therefore, to be possible for Christians (and others) today to be happy and fulfilled as single persons? Perhaps it is time for the church to teach again that singleness is not a condition in any way to be despised.

A choice of attitude

Those choosing to be single in order to serve God more effectively, such as ministers and missionaries who know being unmarried will give them a flexibility and freedom for service, are certainly a minority. Many others find themselves 'single by circumstance' and they have to learn to cope with a condition

---

[1] Stanley Grenz, *Sexual Ethics*, Word Publishing, Dallas, 1990, p. 167.

which is not of their choice. They have deep longings to have a sexual partner and to have children of their own. Most of all, they long to love and be loved. But the opportunity for marriage to the right person has never come their way.

The choice that single Christians must make is to reject the attitude of the world, and to adopt the attitude of Jesus Christ himself. He calls his followers to be renewed in their minds and to think as he thinks. He offers an alternative lifestyle. The danger for believers always is that we subconsciously adopt the world's culture and take on board the way unbelievers live. Christians who are single, therefore, must choose to think as Christ thought.

Not enough has been done, or is being done, by the churches to help single Christians to make this choice of a positive attitude towards singleness. Let me develop further what I mean.

The church family

First, single Christians do belong to a family and this needs to become more of a reality in the churches' ongoing life. It is true that some single people feel very much at home in their church fellowship; but there are many who not only do not feel at home in their churches but do not have a strong family structure to support them. Into this category come many divorcees, those with a homosexual orientation and many widow(er)s.

The Bible's theology of the church is based on a spiritual family with God as Father, the church as mother and Christ as our elder Brother. But few congregations make an effort to work out this theology into their ongoing programmes. The Church needs to work hard at providing the kind of family structure which will support and embrace the single people within its fellowship.

I am thinking of some very simple practical measures such as hospitality on the Lord's Day, church holidays (not necessarily formally arranged, but families within the congregation including single people in their plans). The kind of holidays which are arranged particularly for single people can actually be very unhelpful. It can be a great strain for several dozen singles to be thrown together for a week of fortnight. Many prefer to be part of a family where there are children. Few Christians ever think of inviting their single friends to share in the family experience.

Children

The mention of children leads to a second point. Many who are single would appreciate greatly becoming close to a family with children, and being trusted to entertain the children on a regular basis to days out, or to meals or tea-parties in the single person's home. The 'aunt' or 'uncle' figure can be most important and helpful in a child's development. But how few Christians have ever thought of adopting a single person in their fellowship to be an 'aunt' or 'uncle' to their children. At least some of those who have no children of their own would greatly appreciate the opportunity to be able to care for children at a deep level.

Sexuality does not mean sexual relationships

Third, the common misunderstanding of our society today is to confuse sexual activity and sexuality. But these two are not the same. Our sexuality is our essential masculinity or femininity. Men and women were created by God to be exactly complementary. It is certainly true that this complementarity is both symbolized and expressed within marriage by sexual union. But that is only one aspect of sexuality. Men and women can enjoy their sexuality without sexual union.

They can work together and appreciate and benefit from the sexuality of the other in business or professional relationships.

For sixteen years of my own ministry, I worked with a pastoral team which included both men and women. I found that I benefited immensely from the female members of the team just as much as from the male members. The women tended to think more relationally than the men. They had a particular contribution to make without which the team would been very much the poorer.

In such working relationships, when the sexuality of each one finds full expression, and when that expression is appreciated and valued by the others, there will be both enjoyment and fulfillment. The work will prosper and be all the richer for such complementary relationships.

It cannot be denied that men have tended to try and dominate women, with the result that women's sexuality has been repressed and has not been allowed to have full expression. The New Testament's teaching makes it very clear that women had their proper place in the fellowship. The obvious example of this is the partnership in service of Priscilla and Aquila. Men and women have to relearn to respect the other's sexuality and to discover the enormous rewards of working together as partners. Today's feminist movement can introduce an element of rivalry which is far from the harmony there should be in Christ. Men can forestall such competitive rivalry by allowing the women's sexuality to have proper expression within the working relationships of the fellowship.

Sex

Fourth, the Bible's clear prohibition of sexual relationships outside marriage has been misrepresented in our day as narrow-mindedness which represses perfectly natural sexual desires. Why does the Bible take such a strong moral position? What is the meaning of sexual intercourse? Stanley Grenz offers a threefold explanation of sexual union within marriage.[2]

First, the sex act recalls the commitment of husband and wife to each other. It is a kind of re-enactment of their marriage vows and is designed by God to represent and effect the marriage bonding.

Second, sexual intercourse is an act of mutual submission.[3] In this way, husband and

---

[2] *Op. cit.*, pp. 181-2.
[3] Ephesians 5:21.

wife express to each other their desire to please each other. Sex outside a stable relationship of full commitment cannot communicate this vital element of marriage. Indeed, outwith such a stable relationship, sex will either have self-gratification as its goal or else will be a means of manipulating the other partner.

Third, sexual intercourse declares that this relationship is open to another in that procreation is effected through sex. I am not discounting the practice of family planning. But basic to sexual union is this vital possibility of bringing into being another living person in order to develop the union of husband and wife into a family. But in sex outside marriage the partners will do all possible to prevent the intrusion of a child. It follows that marriage is the only proper context for sexual union.

These three meanings of sexual union ought to symbolize the life of every church fellowship. First, the bonding of Christians within the church must be allowed often to re-enact their mutual commitment in Christ's love. Second, that bonding must be characterized by mutual submission. Thirdly, it must give birth to new life as the fellowship's evangelism brings new members into the church's family.

Love

Fifth, single persons need just as much as married people to experience love. Note that the Bible never uses the Greek word *eros*, sexual love. Yet believers are constantly exhorted to show love, whether *agape, storge* or *philia*.[4] Some fellowships are small which can make it easy for those in the 'body of Christ' to care for each other in a loving way. In larger fellowships, however, the tendency will be for people unconsciously to form unofficial groupings. That is where single people can be neglected. It doesn't take much reflection to see that being worked out in most fellowships.

I have noticed the problem especially when a single person tries to find a way into a new fellowship having moved home and job. Friendships and unofficial groups in the church are already well entrenched; single people in the church already have established friendships with other single people. So the

---

[4] *'agape* means 'self-giving love'; *storge* means 'the affection of family love'; *philia* means 'friendship'.

newcomer finds him or herself at a loss to become part of the new fellowship.

How conscious is your fellowship of this problem for single people? How sensitive are you to the deep need for love in the stranger who shyly sits alone as a visitor to your church? What steps do you already take to make that person welcome and quickly become part of a loving, caring, supporting family group? The answers to these questions can at times be desolatingly disappointing!

Single people themselves can have a real sphere of service in every Christian congregation by seeking out lonely people and not only offering friendship and concern, but also going on to integrate them into the life and heart of the church. It often takes selflessness and even sacrifice for other Christians to allow the newcomers to share a place in already existing close groups of friends.

Intimacy

Sixth, as with sexuality, intimacy is often confused with sexual intercourse. So called 'one-night-stands' engage in sex without any intimacy. But many dear friends enjoy deep intimacy without ever engaging in sex. I myself have no doubt from my own pastoral experience that the single person craves more for intimacy than for a sexual relationship.

What is meant by intimacy? Intimacy requires a mutual, deep, personal knowledge between two people which can develop into a strong trust. Those who have such intimacy will often understand what the other person means or thinks just by a glance or picking up facial signals such as a frown or raising of the eyebrows. Those who are intimate will care for each other and will offer faithful criticism ('the wounds of a friend can be trusted' [Proverbs 27:6]) as well as loving encouragement. They will share a common history and mutual memories, and will stand by each other in times of illness or difficulty.

It is sad that some who are single are afraid of this kind of deep, meaningful intimacy. It is possible that because of the deification of sex by today's society, they mistake intimacy for a sexual relationship. But David and Jonathan shared an intimate relationship without any sexual expression whatsoever (see 1 Samuel 18:1ff.; 20:41f.; 23:16ff.; 2 Samuel 1:26).

Postscript

What about the sexual tension and frustration which many single people experience? We have to recognize that even with the love, concern, family involvement and chaste intimacy which we have outlined above, there will nevertheless still be powerful sexual desires which many find it almost impossible to cope with. Modern society with television, radio, films and magazines does much to arouse and stimulate these desires. Harold Smith makes the following comment:

> Single adults must learn to channel their sex drives in a way that will not offend. Thus, what one finds sublimating will be questionable to another. Many single adults find masturbation a subtle sublimation of the sex drives. It re-channels the drive from illicit sexual intercourse. Many singles regard masturbation as the lesser of two evils.[5]

A contrary view is given by Heather Wraight in her excellent little book in which she reminds her readers that Jesus taught the lustful look and thought was in essence as wrong as the actual deed.[6] It is vital that each person works hard at maintaining purity of mind. Every thought must be brought into captivity and be obedient to Christ. Every one of us fails many times in this way, but we

---

[5] Harold Ivan Smith, *Single and Feeling Good*, Abingdon Press, Nashville, 1987, p. 54.

[6] Heather Wraight, *Single the Jesus Model*, Crossway Books, Leicester, 1995, p. 83.

must remember that there is grace to cleanse and forgive each moment of each day, and we must never abandon the fight to keep our hearts pure, as Christ is pure.

Finally, all of us need to be reminded of the dignity that Christ gave to singleness. He took little children in his arms. He shared a home and was welcomed into families such as that of Lazarus, Martha and Mary. He was especially intimate with John whom he loved. At the same time he was a man of great strength who could drive a rabble of cheating traders out of the temple court. None could deny our Lord was fulfilled, though single!

Christ himself must be the pattern for those who for whatever reason find themselves living as singles. Your attitude should be the same as that of Christ Jesus (Philippians 2:5). With his help and in the bosom of his family, the church, we will find it is gloriously possible to live as he would have us live, and so to glorify his name.

Chapter Seven

The Mystery of Marriage

David C. Searle

One of the features of American life in the minds of the British—forgive me if I am wrong—is litigation or court actions. I understand that America has more lawyers than any other of the professions, certainly far more lawyers than clergymen! I have to confess that the United Kingdom is going the same way, and people are increasingly taking court action, claiming compensation for almost anything and everything.

What the views of the Apostle Paul would be on this matter of litigation I wouldn't venture to guess. But if Paul were to take court action against all the theologians who have written about his teaching on marriage, I am quite sure he would win massive compensation for being slandered and misrepresented. What he says is infinitely more balanced and fairer to husbands and wives than many have made out. Let's look at his teaching on marriage in Ephesians 5:21ff.

We will also look briefly at Peter's comments in 1 Peter 3:1-7.

Men and women equal but different

If we look at the history of the human race in general, and the history of marriage in particular, we find that men have been guilty of exploiting women. I don't think there can be any argument about that. In some civilizations, women have been regarded as the chattels of men, little better than skivvies and slaves. That is why the feminist movement has been fighting back so hard in recent years to try and recover the lost dignity of women. Do you know that even God's people, the Jews, have been guilty of this? An orthodox Jews in Jesus' day used to pray each day, 'I thank Thee God that I am neither a Gentile, a dog, nor a woman.'

But what does the Bible say about men and women? We are told in Genesis 1 that God created man and woman in his own image. The man and the woman stood over against everything else that God had made, and were the very crown of God's creation. They stood side by side as equals: 'male and female he created them' (Genesis 1:27c).[1]

---

[1] See Chapter 1, p. 4ff.

Their equality as persons did not mean that they were the same. The woman is called in Genesis 2 a helper suitable for the man. In case some are tempted to think the word 'helper' is rather patronizing, bear in mind this word is only used 21 times in the OT, and 15 of those occurrences use it of God coming to lift up men when they have fallen and are nearly broken, and the Almighty comes to raise them up, give them fresh hope, a new start and renewed strength. So when Genesis 2 calls the woman the man's helper, it is describing her as performing a God-like task for the man. She is actually doing for the man what God also must do for him.[2]

While it is their equality in status that points to their being in God's image, it is their difference in function that distinguishes them from God and reveals they are human, not divine. Their physical make-up tells us that.

But there is an order too, with the man created first, then the woman. The significance of that order in creation spells responsibility on the part of the man as the first-born—his it is to care and provide for the woman.

---

[2] For a fuller explanation of the equality of man and women as taught in Genesis, see Chapter 1, pp. 11-13.

Now all this is in the thinking of Paul when he wrote about marriage as he did in Ephesians 5. Regard Genesis 1 and 2 as ACT 1 in the drama of marriage and give ACT 1 the title of 'Complementarity'. Not until the Christian teaching in Ephesians 5:21ff. and 1 Peter 3:1ff. Do we have ACT 3 of the marriage drama. ACT 2, with the title 'Rivalry', comes between Genesis 2 and Ephesians 5 and is a sorry story. Genesis 3 is where the exploitation begins.

ACT 2 in this drama of marriage begins in Genesis 3 when sin broke into a perfect world and when a curse came upon both the man and his wife. The wife is told that her desire will be for her husband, but he will rule over her. The meaning there is that she will no longer fulfil the complementary role as she should and find complete fulfilment in doing so, but that she will try to dominate her husband, but he will end up dominating her, which is why ACT 2 can be called 'Rivalry'. An unhappy rivalry has characterized the sexes since the Fall, and continues to characterize the sexes. It is not that man and woman are no longer in essence complementary, but rather that sin has brought in this rivalry. We see it all around us. The feminist movement bears witness to it

as women seek to challenge men's exploitation of their sex.

So what are we to call ACT 3 in the Bible's
drama? Ephesians 5 describes the marriage of
Christians and if we gave this 3rd ACT a title it
would be 'In Christ, harmony'. Let's look then
at how harmony can be achieved by a
husband and wife who are in Christ.

Mutual submission of husband and wife

'Submit to one another out of reverence for
Christ' (Ephesians 5:21).

Some translations of the Bible make a
paragraph division after v. 21 of Ephesians 5.
But rightly understood, 'submission' is always
the Christian attitude in relationships. So
really v. 21 acts as a link between what Paul
has been saying to Christians about their
relationships with other believers and what he
is about to say to husbands and wives. In the
microcosm of the family, submission is the
key as it is in the macrocosm of the church.

But however can we square a mutual
submission of husband and wife to each other
with what Paul goes on to say about the wife's
submission to her husband? The answer is not
difficult to find. It is that the role model for
both husband and wife is Christ himself.

(i) *wives*

> Wives, submit to your husbands as to the
> Lord. For the husband is the head of the
> wife as Christ is the head of the church, his
> body, of which is the Saviour. Now as the
> church submits to Christ, so also wives
> should submit to their husbands in
> everything (Ephesians 5:22-24).

Wives are instructed to submit to their
husbands because a husband is the head of
the wife as Christ is the Head of the church.
Note the meaning of the word 'head'. In
Hebrew thinking, the head was not thought of
as the seat of the mind. The mind was
identified as being in the region of the heart or
chest. The head was seen rather as the source
of life. That was why when someone died in
Bible times, ashes were put on the head. The
thought was that the spark of life had been
extinguished and so ashes, the remnants of a
fire that has burned itself out, were put on the
head. Christ is the Head of the church in that
he is the source of the church's life. Our life
flows from him, and only flows from him as
we are joined to him as part of the Body (that
is, the church) of which he is Head. He not
only sustains us, but bears responsibility for
us.

In the same way, the husband is head of the wife. Headship cannot mean that the husband does all the thinking. Not at all. It is in the realm of thinking that the mutual submission comes in. What headship means is leadership, or captaincy. A captain of a team is given that role by the other members of the team. The captain doesn't normally seek that role. He is elected to it. It is the team's gift to him and it is his responsibility to lead the team. In order to be captain of his team, he must have the support of the team members. The captain may not even be the best member of the team. But as captain, he must lead.

So the wife must give her husband the captaincy of the marriage team. Unless she freely gives him that role, rivalry and friction will result. But why should she give him the place and responsibility of being head? Because Christ is her role model. He sub-mitted to his Father. That is not to say he is not equal with the Father. Of course he is. The three Persons of the Trinity of God are co-equal. But, as Paul tells us in Philippians 5, Christ did not see equality as something to be grasped, but submitted gladly and joyfully to his Father's will and became a human being for us that he might become our Saviour. He remained equal with the Father as Son of God.

But he submitted in meekness to the Father's will.

Now that is how wives should submit to their husbands. Their submission to their husbands is in fact submission to the Lord. They are called on to be Christlike in their relationships with their husbands. So wives, your husbands cannot fulfil their role in marriage unless you help them to do so by electing them captain of your marriage team. That is the first step on the pathway to harmony in marriage.

(b) *husbands*

> Husbands, love your wives, just as Christ loved the church and gave himself up for her to make her holy, cleansing her by the washing with water through the word, and to present her to himself as a radiant church, without stain or wrinkle or any other blemish, but holy and blameless. In this same way, husbands ought to love their wives as their own bodies. He who loves his wife loves himself. After all, no-one ever hated his own body, but he feeds and cares for it, just as Christ does the church (Ephesians 5:25-29).

We have just seen that Christ is the role model for *both* husband and wife. So how is Christ the model for the husband? Paul tells us.

Christ loved his bride to such an extent that he laid down his life for her and died to be her Saviour. His love was a lavish, selfless, sacrificial love. That is how husbands are to love their wives, with a sacrificial, self-giving love.

Yes, husbands and wives are to share together, to work together, to plan together. Men must listen to their wives and must then take responsibility for decisions. They must take action which does not consider primarily their own interests, but the interests of their wives and children in the light of God's commands. They are to do this because they love them.

I have been in pastoral ministry for forty-three years. In all the marriage counselling in which I have been engaged, I have never once heard a wife complain that her husband loved her too much. The interesting thing is that Paul says nothing to wives about loving their husbands. Why not? The answer is easy. When a woman is truly, sacrificially loved, she will respond and love in return.

So Paul sees the way to end rivalry between a husband and wife as being in the balance of wifely submission to her husband's leadership—and don't forget, it is primarily a submission to the Lord Jesus Christ—and the

husband's lavish, sacrificial love of his wife by
which he loves her and loves her and loves
her.

Husbands, how does Christ love us? Does
his love for us have any limits? Does the Lord
hold our sins and shortcomings against us?
Does he ever reject us because we fail him, or
don't come up to standard? Not at all! Does
Christ not love us, and forgive us, and keep
on loving us, in spite of all our shortcomings
and turning from him? Freely, bountifully, he
loves. His love cannot be measured. It is
higher, wider, deeper than the measure of our
human intellects. That is how those who are
husbands must love their wives. And that is
the pathway to harmony in a marriage.

The glamorous wife and the considerate husband

We move from Ephesians 5 to 1 Peter 3:1-7.
Peter takes a very similar line to Paul in his
instructions to wives and husbands, but there
is a significant difference in what he says to
wives. The reason is that Peter is addressing
women whose husbands are not believers.
These wives have become Christians after
marriage, and Peter is concerned that they do
their best to win their husbands for Christ.

Echoing Paul, he tells them the best way to do this is by submission.

(a) *the glamorous wife*

> Wives, in the same way be submissive to your husbands so that, if any of them do not believe the word, they may be won over without words by the behaviour of their wives, when they see the purity and reverence of your lives. Your beauty should not come from outward adornment, such as braided hair and the wearing of gold jewellery and fine clothes. Instead, it should be that of your inner self, the unfading beauty of a gentle and quiet spirit, which is of great worth in God's sight. For this is the way the holy women of the past who put their hope in God used to make themselves beautiful. They were submissive to their own husbands, like Sarah, who obeyed Abraham and called him her master. You are her daughters if you do what is right and do not give way to fear (1 Peter 3:1–6).

Negatively, Peter tells wives not to preach at their husbands. A Christian wife will not normally win her husband to Christ if she lectures him. The way to win a man, says Peter, is by your behaviour. Let your life speak. He mentions three aspects of a Christian wife's life, and we will look at just one of the three: first, her purity; second, her reverence; third, her beauty. Consider the third point Peter makes, a woman's beauty.

A Christian wife, to be a good wife, must be a glamorous wife. Christian women should be stunningly beautiful. And Peter lists several ways in which this can be done. He mentions hairstyling, make-up, jewellery and clothes. But he says that in all of these a Christian wife should be extremely modest. Costly jewellery, expensive hairstyles, the latest in cosmetics and the most fashionable designer clothes are exactly what I do not mean by glamour, says Peter. What I do mean by glamour, he says, is a beautiful spirit that shines out from the heart.

I was recently in Brazil and visited some of the most deprived slum areas I have ever seen in my life. I spoke in two churches situated in these areas. I met some of the most beautiful people I have seen. Their clothes were poor and worn, yet clean and neatly mended. But the radiance, grace and glory shining from their faces was very striking. Several times as I climbed into the ramshackle car that was to take me on to my next engagement, my cheeks were wet from my tears, so moved was I after meeting and greeting these humble folk. I had seen the likeness of Jesus Christ reflected in their faces and that clear reflection moved me very deeply.

Now that is the glamour Peter is speaking about. Not an outward glamour from a bottle or from expensive clothes or jewellery or coiffured hair, but an inner beauty. For the condition of our hearts will reflect itself on our faces.

Peter is not saying that Christian wives should be dowdy, and not bother with their appearance. What he is saying is that the glamour, the attractiveness that will count for Jesus Christ comes from inside. It cannot be put on artificially.

(b) *the considerate husband*

> Husbands, in the same way be considerate as you live with your wives, and treat them with respect as the weaker partner and as heirs with you of the gracious gift of life, so that nothing will hinder your prayers (1 Peter 3:7).

'In the same way' means that the principles Peter has just laid down for the wife of submission and grace apply equally to the husband. When he says, 'as heirs with you [or, together] of the gracious gift of life', he is referring to the equality of the man and woman as standing side by side, created in God's image.

But husbands should notice the word 'considerate'. Peter is saying that husbands should always think of their wives. They should respect them, and not 'do them down'. Men can sometimes be sarcastic about their wives when in company. Of course, there is a jocular way of speaking and many husbands are sometimes guilty of that. But it is easy to show lack of respect for one's wife and so to show lack of loving consideration for them.

Two reasons are given why husbands must be considerate in this tender, loving way. The first is that the woman is different from the man. Physically, emotionally and relationally, she is different. Recognize those differences, respect and honour those differences. A wife needs special consideration because hers is the role of bearing children, caring for them and nurturing them in their early years. It is true husbands should play their full part in that task, but the wife has a deeper, more internal way of relating to her children. She needs her husband, but she needs him to be particularly considerate to her in all she is called on to do and be as a woman.

The second reason given for special consideration is that husband and wife stand together, side by side, in the presence of God, cleansed by Christ, loved and redeemed by him, made members together of his Father's family, and accepted by grace that is boundless and free. While physically and emotionally she is different, she is nonetheless a joint heir with her husband of the gracious gift of life.

The practical application of 'In Christ, harmony'

Now can we gather all this together? How are we getting along in our marriages? What I mean is, how do our marriages compare with God's pattern for husbands and wives? Follow through for just a moment ACT 1, 2 and 3. ACT 1 played out in Genesis 1 and 2: Complementarity. I hope it's not too facile to ask if we have grasped that complementary nature of our relationship, that men and women are equal in status, but different in function. There is a great deal of modern rubbish talked about this, you know. Feminism recognizes the equality, but tends to lose sight of the difference. Men and women are not the same. If we were the same, then gay and lesbian relationships would be alright. But we are different in a fundamental and vital way which makes a man and woman exactly complementary to each other in a way which homosexual relationships lack—they do not have that complementary difference and that is why their relationships will always be flawed. A man and woman need each other, and make together the perfect pair; two halves of the apple! So, have we recognized the wonder of ACT 1?

ACT 2 and the action begins in Genesis 3: Rivalry. It may be that reading this is the one ideal couple in a million! Very occasionally I have met couples who have told me they have never had a cross word in forty years of marriage. Well, my wife and I can't say that! I suspect that if we are honest, most of us have to admit we have often experienced that uneasy rivalry which comes as a result of the Fall. A tension as the wife tries to persuade her husband to listen to her and the husband is foolishly determined to do his own thing and ignore his wife's interests and wishes.

Many marriages have a dark shadow over them, and only rarely does the sun shine on them from a cloudless sky. Sadly, there are too many shaky marriages among Christian people today. There are marriages in which grudges being harboured. At times communication breaks down and tensions develop; attitudes and prejudices which lack both understanding and submission become the norm of daily living.

Maybe the rivalry arises from stolen love. A partner's love has been given to another, and is not wholly given to the wife or husband. And so rivalry is sharp, even bitter. ACT 2 is being played out in that marriage and the consequences are unhappiness for both husband and wife and insecurity for their children. It is high time to close the curtain on ACT 2 and usher in ACT 3 as described by Paul in Ephesians 5:21ff.: In Christ, harmony.

Harmony, as both husband and wife make Christ himself their role model. Mutual submission, with the wife giving her husband the place of head as her special 'wedding gift', and the husband lavishing his wife with sacrificial love. Harmony because the wife's concern is inner beauty, the beauty of a godly life, and the husband's concern is to be considerate and give his wife the utmost respect and honour.

So, how is ACT 3 going? I have my wife's permission to write this: we met when we were both 17, and dated each other for six years before we married at age 23. We soon discovered that we were possibly the most incompatible pair that ever married. So our marriage has not been easy. Most of the fault has been on my side. But over the years, I have been learning some insights into the mystery of how marriage can work and be harmonious. Those insights come from God's Word. And I believe I can say that today we must be among the happiest married couples living in Scotland. After 45 years as husband and wife, we are deeply in love, more deeply in love than ever, and harmony is the keynote of our lives. Not that it is always easy, but that it is gloriously possible, and we prove it every day.

So how about you? Take the Word of God seriously. Wives, dare to submit to your husbands, as you submit to the Lord. Husbands, guard your hearts and save your love exclusively for your wives and just heap that love on them, not in ostentatious ways, but from deep within. Love them and love them and love them! Remember that love is not foremost an emotion, but an act of the will, an act of obedience to Christ. We love, because he first loved us.

Chapter Eight

Homosexuality and Health

Trevor Stammers[1]

This chapter gives a brief overview of research relating to homosexual practice and health. It does not seek to draw moral judgments from biology but aims to make clear what current medical literature indicates are the health consequences of homosexual sex for both men and women.

Sexually Transmitted Infections

Non-HIV Infections

In the UK, non-HIV sexual infections far outweigh numbers of infections with HIV. The total number of new diagnoses seen in GUM (genito-urinary medicine) clinics rose by 3% from 768,339 in 2004 to 790,387 in 2005.[2] The total of new HIV diagnoses for the UK in 2004 was 7271,[3] only 0.9% of the total new STI diagnoses.

The Health Protection Agency report for 2005 highlights a 'worrying situation with undiminished and high levels of transmission of HIV and other sexually transmitted infections (STIs) among men who have sex with men (MSM)....'[4]

MSM are the first group in the report's section on 'Groups Requiring Targeted Prevention'.[5] The excess risk posed to MSM is clearly shown in reference to many non-HIV STIs, as the following extracts indicate:

- diagnoses of syphilis in the UK among MSM remain relatively high, accounting for 54% (1062/1977) of the total diagnoses among all men in 2004, and are the result of ongoing outbreaks in Manchester, Brighton, London and other UK cities;[6] in 2000 the number of diagnoses of syphilis in MSM was 130, rising to 1062 in 2004[7]

- 215 cases of lymphogranuloma venereum (LGV) were confirmed in the UK up to the end of September 2005, reflecting an outbreak in MSM, many of whom were co-infected with HIV;[8] the *British Medical Journal* commented on this outbreak that 'As in the rest of Europe, all UK cases have occurred in men who have sex with men who are predominantly white and HIV positive (80%); infection has been associated with high risk sexual behaviours including unprotected anal intercourse and 'fisting" (insertion of a hand into the rectum)'[9]

- diagnoses of gonorrhoea in MSM increased by 27% from 3140 in 2000 to 3977 in 2004[10]

HIV Infections

• cumulatively, the majority of HIV infections reported to the Centre For Infections have occurred through sex between men. Within the UK, this group remains at greatest risk of acquiring HIV infection; there has been no evidence in recent years of a decline in the numbers of new infections in this group and over 1800 new diagnoses of HIV are currently occurring each year[11]

• London has been the main focus of the HIV epidemic in the UK; 55% percent of those infected through sex between men live in London[12]

The above statistics should all be considered in the light of the fact that only 2.6% of men in the UK have reported having sex with other men with the past 5 years.[13]

Lesbian Sex and STIs

Though sexually-active lesbians may intuitively be thought to be at low risk of STIs, this does not seem actually to be the case.[14,15] In one study, lesbian women were 4.5 times more likely to have had more than 50 lifetime partners than heterosexual women and 93% of lesbians reported having sex with men, many of whom were high risk of HIV infection themselves.[16] Lesbian women are also at risk of non-HIV infections including herpes[17] and human papillomavirus,[18] the principal cause of cervical cancer.

Risks of Anal Intercourse

Though also practised by heterosexuals, anal sex is the *sine qua non* of sex for many MSM. The lining of the rectum, unlike the vagina, is predominantly composed of columnar epithelium and is more prone to tear following trauma. This increases the likelihood of transmission of infection. In one study of MSM, 70% of acts of anal intercourse overall and 40% of such acts by HIV positive men, were unprotected.[19]

Anal Cancer

It has been known for a long time that 'homosexual behaviour in men is a risk factor for anal cancer'.[20] The whole pattern of incidence of anal cancer has now changed and whereas it used to be more frequent in women, the sex incidence is now almost equal.[21] Though smoking is an important risk factor for the developement of anal cancer, 90% are linked with human papillomavirus infection and gay or bisexual orientation and a history of ano-receptive intercourse are well-recognised risk factors.[22]

Intestinal Infections

'Intestinal infections… now commonly occur among homosexually active men. Frequently referred to as the "gay bowel syndrome", recent studies have shown a high incidence of enteric pathogens… among homosexual men.'[23] Though the use of term 'gay bowel sydrome' suddenly dropped from the medical literature from the early 1990s,[24] concern about atypical bowel infections in MSM remains.[25]

Anal Trauma and Incontinence

'There is a rising trend in high risk sexual behaviour among men who have sex with men (MSM), with concomitant use of recreational drugs. Activities include fisting and unprotected anal intercourse with a partner who is HIV serodiscordant or of unknown status.'[26] Such activities can lead to perforation of the rectum or even the colon.[27]

The first published study on the effect of ano-receptive intercourse indicated that it was a risk factor for anal incontinence, with 14 out of 40 MSM suffering from such incontinence;[28] a later study did not show an increased risk of incontinence with ano-receptive intercourse however.[29]

Mental Health

The evidence that MSM have more mental ill-health than heterosexuals is so overwhelming that even advocates of homosexual sex acknowledge it to be so.[30,31] This applies to anxiety, depression, suicide attempts and drug dependence.[32,33,34,35,36] The only paper I could locate claiming that the psychological well-being of MSM is the same as heterosexual men, actually showed it to be the same as divorced and single men (both high risk groups for mental disorder).[37] Lesbian women are also at excess lifetime risk of depression, suicide and drug and alcohol dependence.[38,39,40]

The usual explanation proposed is that 'in response to the external pressure and isolation they often face, lesbian and gay young people are more vulnerable than others to psychosocial problems'.[41] This claim is totally unreferenced however and is unsupported by other data demonstrating that:

• the excess mental health risk of MSM and WSW persists in both countries with liberal (e.g. Canada) and less liberal (e.g. USA) homosexual legislation[42]

• 'Societal discrimination inadequately accounts for these differences since parallel comparisons of blacks and whites produced a pattern unlike the differences found between homosexuals and non-homosexuals'[43]

• bisexuals are at even higher risk of mental ill-health than homosexuals or heterosexuals[44]

• substance misuse seems linked to the process of 'coming out' rather than 'gay-related stressful life events'[45]

• much of the recreational drug use, especially of amyl nitrates ('poppers') is to facilitate or enhance sexual pleasure[46,47,48,49] and has nothing to do with social approval or disapproval

This does not in any way excuse or minimize the harmful impact of verbal or other abuse of gay and lesbian people[50,51]. 'Homosexuals shouldn't have to suffer their doctors' prejudices'[52] or anyone else's. However this is a far cry from responsible evidence-based health education. There is no empirical support for 'those championing homosexual rights based upon the argument that there are no real differences between those who indulge and those who do not'.[53] Anyone who has spent a Saturday night on call in a metropolitan casualty department knows the truth of that.

Editor's Additional Note

It should also be added that the United Kingdom is experiencing an epidemic of heterosexual diseases. Figures released in 2006 by the Health Protection Agency show a 20% increase in STIs since 2005. In the early 1990s, it was thought that syphillis had been virtually eradicated, but in the 12 months prior to the latest reports, it is seen to have increased by 25%. (Over the ten years prior to 2005, there was a 750% increase in syphillis in women aged 16 to 19 years, and 1500% increase in women aged 45 to 64 years.) In the past 12 months, there have also been sharp rises among women aged 45 to 64 years in other STIs: gonorrhea by 115%, chlamydia by 218%, herpes by 65% and genital warts by 30%. STIs among heterosexual men also continue to rise. It is tempting to conclude that if society still adhered to traditional Christian moral values, much pain and heartache would be avoided.

Endnotes

[1] Dr Trevor Stammers, B.Sc., FRCGP, DRCOG, DPAB, Senior Tutor in General Practice, St George's, University of London.

[2] Health Protection Agency Sexually Transmitted Infection Data 2005:
www.hpa.org.uk/infections/topics_az/hiv_and_sti/epidemiology/sti_data.htm

[3] www.hpa.org.uk/infections/topics_az/hiv_and_sti/hiv/epidemiology/hars_tables.htm#country

[4] www.hpa.org.uk/publications/2005/hiv_sti_2005/execsummary.htm

[5] www.hpa.org.uk/publications/2005/hiv_sti_2005/msm.htm

[6] www.hpa.org.uk/publications/2005/hiv_sti_2005/msm.htm

[7] www.hpa.org.uk/publications/2005/hiv_sti_2005/pdf/MtI_BW_Part_4_MSM.pdf

[8] www.hpa.org.uk/publications/2005/hiv_sti_2005/msm.htm

[9] Collins L, White JA , Bradbeer C Lymphogranuloma venereum *BMJ* 2006, 332:66.

[10] www.hpa.org.uk/publications/2005/hiv_sti_2005/pdf/Mtl_BW_Part_4_MSM.pdf

[11] www.hpa.org.uk/infections/topics_az/hiv_and_sti/hiv/epidemiology/epidemiology.htm

[12] Ibid.

[13] Johnson A, Mercer C, Erens B, *et al*, 'Sexual Behaviour in Britain: partnerships, practices, and HIV risk behaviours', *Lancet* 2001, 358:1835-1842.

[14] Marrazzo J M, Coffey P, Elliott M N, 'Sexual practices, risk perception and knowledge of sexually transmitted disease risk among lesbian and bisexual women', *Perspectives on Sexual & Reproductive Health*, 2005, 537:6-12.

[15] Marrazzo JM, 'Barriers to infectious disease care among Lesbians', *Emerging Infectious Diseases*, 2004, 10:1974-1978.

[16] Fethers K, Marks C, Mindel A, Estcourt CS, 'Sexually transmitted infections and risk behaviours in women who have sex with women', *Sex Trans Infections* 2000, 76:345-349.

[17] Marrazzo JM, Stine K, Wald A, 'Prevalence and risk factors for infection with herpes simplex virus type-1 and -2 among lesbians', *Sexually Transmitted Diseases*, 2003, 30:890-895.

[18] Marrazzo JM, Stine K, Koutsky LA, 'Genital human papillomavirus infection in women who have sex with women: a review', *American Journal of Obstetrics & Gynecology*, 2000, 183:770-774.

[19] McManus TJ, 'Sexual behaviour of men' (letter), *BMJ*, 1995, 311:1163.

[20] Daling JR, Weiss NS, Hislop TG *et al*, 'Sexual practices, STDs and the incidence of anal cancer', *NEJM*, 1987, 973-977.

[21] Johnson LG, Madeleine MM, Newcomer LM, Schwartz SM, Daling JR, 'Anal cancer incidence and survival: the surveillance, epidemiology, and end results experience 1973-2000', *Cancer*, 2004, 101:281-288.

[22] Daling JR, Madeleine MM, Johnson LG, Schwartz SM, Shera KA, Wurscher MA, Carter JJ, Porter PL, Galloway DA, McDougall JK, 'Human papillomavirus, smoking, and sexual practices in the etiology of anal cancer', *Cancer*, 2004, 101:270-280.

[23] Quinn TC, 'Clinical approach to intestinal infections in homosexual men', *Med Clinic of N America*, 1986, 70:611-634.

[24] Scarce M, 'Harbinger of plague: a bad case of gay bowel syndrome' *Journal of Homosexuality*, 1997, 34:1-35.

[25] Williams D, Churchill D, 'Ulcerative proctitis in men who have sex with men: an emerging outbreak', *BMJ*, 2006, 332:99-100.

[26] Cohen CE, Giles A, Nelson A, 'Sexual trauma associated with fisting and recreational drugs', *Sex Transm Infect*, 2004, 80:469-470.

[27] Spears K, Hutson H, Atluri S, 'Rectal perforation following manual-anal intercourse' *Acad Emerg Med*, 1995, 2:852–853.

[28] Miles AJ, Allen-Mersh TG, Wastell C, 'Effect of anoreceptive intercourse on anorectal function', *Journal of the Royal Society of Medicine*, 1993, 86:144-147.

[29] Chun AB, Rose S, Mitrani C, Silvestre AJ, Wald A, 'Anal sphincter structure and function in homosexual males engaging in anoreceptive intercourse', *American Journal of Gastro-enterology*, 1997, 92:465-468.

[30] Bagley CD, Augelli AR, 'Suicidal behaviour in gay, lesbian and bisexual youth', *BMJ*, 2000, 320:1617-1618.

[31] Meacher P, 'Psychiatric disorders and risky sexual behaviour' (letter), *BMJ*, 2001, 111-112.

[32] Jorm AF, Korten AE, Rodgers B *et al*, 'Sexual orientation and mental health: results from a community

survey of young and middle-aged adults' *Br J Psych*, 2002, 423-427.

[33] Sandfort TGM, de Graf R, Bijl RV, Schnabel P, 'Same-sex sexual behaviour and psychiatric disorders', *Arch Gen Psych*, 2001, 58:85-91.

[34] Bagley C, Trembaly P, 'Suicidal behaviours in homosexual and bisexual males', *Crisis*, 1997, 24-33.

[35] Cochran SD, Ackerman D, Mays VM, Ross MW, 'Prevalence of non-medical drug use and dependence among homosexually active men and women in the US population', *Addiction*, 2004, 99:989-998.

[36] Stall R, Paul JP, Greenwood G, Pollack LM, Bein E, Crosby GM, Mills TC, Binson D, Coates TJ, Catania JA, 'Alcohol use, drug use and alcohol-related problems among men who have sex with men: the Urban Men's Health Study', *Addiction*, 2001, 96:1589-1601.

[37] Coyle A, 'A study of the psychological well-being among gay men using the GHQ-30', *Br J of Clin Psychol*, 1993, 32:218-220.

[38] Cochran SD, Keenan C, Schober C, Mays VM, 'Estimates of alcohol use and clinical treatment needs among homosexually active men and women in the U.S. population', *Journal of Consulting & Clinical Psychology*, 2000, 68:1062-1071.

[39] Bergmark KH, 'Drinking in the Swedish gay and lesbian community', *Drug & Alcohol Dependence*, 1999, 56:133-143.

[40] Endnotes [33, 35] above.

[41] Endnote [31] above.

[42] Mathy R, 'Homosexual related legislation does not reduce suicidal intent in sexual minority groups' (letter), *BMJ*, 2002, 1176.

[43] Cameron P, Landess T, Cameron K, 'Homosexual sex as harmful as drug abuse, prostitution or smoking', *Psychological Reports*, 2005, 96:915-961.

[44] Endnote [32] above.

[45] Rosario M, Schrimshaw EW, Hunter J, 'Predictors of substance use over time among gay, lesbian and bisexual youths: an examination of three hypotheses', *Addictive Behaviors*, 2004, 29:1623-1631.

[46] Purcell DW, Wolitski RJ, Hoff CC, Parsons JT, Woods WJ, Halkitis PN, 'Predictors of the use of viagra, testosterone and antidepressants among HIV-seropositive gay and bisexual men', *AIDS*, 2005, 19 Suppl., 1:S57-66.

[47] Colfax G, Vittinghoff E, Husnik MJ, McKirnan D, Buchbinder S, Koblin B, Celum C, Chesney M, Huang Y, Mayer K, Bozeman S, Judson FN, Bryant KJ, Coates TJ, EXPLORE Study Team, 'Substance use and sexual risk: a participant- and episode-level analysis among a cohort of men who have sex with men', *American Journal of Epidemiology*, 2004, 159:1002-1012.

[48] Woody GE, VanEtten-Lee ML, McKirnan D, Donnell D, Metzger D, Seage G 3rd, Gross M, HIVNET VPS 001 Protocol Team, 'Substance use among men who have sex with men: comparison with a national household survey', *Journal of Acquired Immune Deficiency Syndromes: JAIDS*, 2001, 27:86-90.

[49] Ross MW, Mattison AM, Franklin DR Jr, 'Club drugs and sex on drugs are associated with different motivations for gay circuit party attendance in men', *Substance Use & Misuse*, 2003, 38:1173-1183.

[50] Hershberger SL, D'Augelli AR, 'The impact of victimization on the mental health and suicidality of lesbian, gay and bisexual youths', *Dev Psychology*, 1995, 65-74.

[51] Savin-Williams R, 'Verbal and physical abuse as stressor in the lives of lesbian, gay males and bisexual youths: associations with school problems, running away, substance abuse, prostitution and suicide', *J Cons and Clinical Psychol*, 1994, 261-269.

[52] McColl P, 'Homosexuality and mental health services', *BMJ*, 1994, 550-551.

[53] Endnote [41] above.

Chapter Nine

The Christian Faith and Homosexuality[1]

David F. Wright

Some people outside the church cannot understand what all the fuss is about. So long as you are responsible and avoid harming others, surely your sexual behaviour is up to you? It is no one else's business what you get up to in the privacy of your bedroom. If sex between a boy and a girl is lawful in Britain at the age of sixteen, why should it be any different for two boys, or two girls? Why not simple equality, in line with basic human rights? In any case, homosexual intercourse is only natural, is it not, for gays and lesbians? Their homosexual identity is part of the 'givenness' of their personal being, rather than a matter of free choice. It is their 'nature', many would claim, and not merely their preferred life-style.

---

[1] This chapter is a shortened version of David Wright's booklet published by Rutherford House in 1994 (2nd edition, 1997) and is used by permission.

Yet for most Christians—to say nothing of Jews and Muslims—the issues are not quite so straightforward. They cannot regard homosexual acts, even within stable relationships, as no more problematic than heterosexual ones. Talk of marriage between gays or between lesbians, on a par with the union of husband and wife, is quite unacceptable. No less inconceivable for most Christians is the appointment to positions of responsibility in the church of individuals who want to engage in same-sex conduct. This is not to deny that intimate male-to-male and female-to-female relationships may be marked by depths of love and care. It is rather to maintain that sex between two males, or between two females, is profoundly unnatural in the Christian scheme of things—that is to say, it is contrary to God's will for human life.

Christian Convictions under Pressure

This widespread Christian conviction—until recently, the universal Christian conviction— is under pressure for various reasons today One very obvious reason is the diminishing respect for the Christian faith in contemporary society and culture. This is most evident in many sections of the media, and is related to the sharp decline in membership of the mainstream churches over the last three or four decades. For some churchmen, especially in churches that have traditionally enjoyed national status, this retreat into a minority position (and one that is increasingly despised or ridiculed) is very uncomfortable and embarrassing. For many of them it has become a high priority to revise Christian beliefs, in an endeavour to retain or recover Christian credibility in a world that seems increasingly disinterested in the church and its teaching. Not surprisingly, some are ready to jettison central elements in the world-wide Christian tradition's sexual ethics.

Avoiding prejudice

Another reason why some are proposing a drastic recasting of Christian teaching in this area is a sense of shame or guilt at past persecution of homosexuals—and, we might add, at the continuing currency of deep-seated, irrational prejudice against the whole subject. Recently this has been called the 'Yuk-factor', an unthinking distaste, even nausea, at any suggestion of same-sexuality. It expresses more a gut-reaction than a reasoned and responsible attitude. Too many Christians find the very mention of genital homosexual activity so repugnant that they cannot talk about it among themselves. Such an aversion is sometimes called 'homophobia'. Although it may point to the submerged promptings of an authentic Christian instinct, it cannot do service for a considered Christian judgment which has to spell out the whys and wherefores.

In the interest of clarity and charity, the word 'homophobia' is best avoided altogether. Most phobias, like agoraphobia (dread of open spaces), for example, are conditions that sufferers need treatment for. It is increasingly common for any disapproval, however reasonable and considered, of active homosexuality to be labelled homophobic. The word simply sours discussion.

Nor should Christians be swayed overmuch by links between homosexuality and other sicknesses in our society, such as violence, promiscuity, prostitution, child-abuse and sexually transmitted infections. After all, predominantly heterosexual populations have produced plenty of each of these down the ages! It is true that some surveys have shown male homosexuals to have many more partners than heterosexuals (and some gay advocates openly argue that promiscuity is intrinsic to their life-style). Yet rampant sexual licence of itself does not discredit all expressions of heterosexuality; it alone does not settle the deepest questions about homosexuality.

In this connection we would do well to avoid altogether the use of the term 'sodomy'. There was undoubtedly a homosexual element in the Sodomites' attempted violation of Lot's guests (Genesis 19:1-11), but their abominable behaviour had much more to it and—to judge from references to the episode later in the Old Testament—much worse to it than that. Not only was it gang-rape, it was a grave breach of the sacred duty of hospitality. To call all male homosexuals 'sodomites is a quite unpardonable slur.

Facing the key question

Christians must face the moral challenge of homosexuality at its strongest. The question in essence is this: would homosexual behaviour be acceptable if it satisfied all the other conditions that acceptable heterosexual behaviour has to meet in Christian teaching? That is to say, might there be an approved homosexual equivalent to the lifelong sexual binding of husband and wife in marriage?

For believers in most Christian churches, who accept that God's Word in Scripture is the supreme rule of faith and life, the answer must be sought there. The Bible has few explicit references to homosexual practices, but all of them are unambiguously disapproving. The main evidence will be set out below. Some would argue today that, for one reason or another, the biblical accounts are largely irrelevant to contemporary realities, but none can deny that, in their own terms, the Christian Scriptures invariably and uncompromisingly depict homosexual acts in an unfavourable light.[2]

Why so few references in Scripture?

But why are they so rarely mentioned? One obvious answer is that homosexual behaviour did not often occur within Old Testament Israel or the New Testament church. It was not a common problem. In the restricted space of this brief account, it is enough to note that homosexuality has not been a universal feature of human history. In this respect we should not regard modern Western society as typical of all other cultures and periods of civilisation.

Another reason why the biblical mentions of homosexual acts are so few and so brief

---

[2] Some of David Wright's original treatment of the biblical references to homosexuality have been omitted since they are dealt with in chapters 1 and 2 of this book

and often incidental is that they were self-evidently reprehensible. There is no evidence whatsoever that Israel or early Judaisim or primitive Christianity needed any debate to determine whether the homosexual phenomena they encountered were displeasing to God. If this issue was not a big one in the apostolic churches (or among the Old Testament people of God), this was not because they could not make up their minds about it, or thought that it did not really matter one way or the other. It was an open-and shut case. They apparently did not reckon it unloving or intolerant to condemn the forms of homosexuality they met with.

The big Issue: the matching of male and female

The underlying reason for this uniform and unquestioning biblical attitude is writ large in the Scriptures. It is a principle of enormous importance—that the difference between male and female and the sexual matching of male and female are grounded in the gift and purpose of God our Creator. Men and women are made to find sexual fulfilment with each other. (See Chapter 1 above.)

The Genesis account of creation undergirds the whole biblical story of God's dealings with humankind. It is truly fundamental, as we see elsewhere in the Scriptures.

Jesus himself directed some Pharisees to these biblical foundations set out in Genesis 1 and 2 when they questioned him about the grounds for divorce:

> Jesus replied, 'But at the beginning of creation God "made them male and female... For this reason a man will leave his father and mother and be united to his wife, and the two will become one flesh." So they are no longer two, but one. Therefore what God has joined together, let not man separate' (Mark 10:6-9).

This biblical charter for male-female relations is widely reflected and echoed and alluded to. Three of the Ten Commandments assume it:

> Honour your father and your mother... You shall not commit adultery. You shall not covet your neighbour's wife....

A Reflection of God's Relation to his People

Both in the Old Testament and in the New, this one-flesh union of man and woman, is used as a pattern of the supreme relationship open to human beings—the union between God and his people. So the prophet Jeremiah speaks in the name of the Lord:

> 'Return, faithless people', declares the Lord, 'for I am your husband... But like a woman

unfaithful to her husband, so you have been
unfaithful to me, O house of Israel'
(Jeremiah 3:14, 20—and the whole chapter).

In a beautiful and moving account of his
wooing of Jerusalem God speaks through
Ezekiel as follows:

'[W]hen I looked at you and saw that you
were old enough for love, I spread the
corner of my garment over you and covered
your nakedness. I gave you my solemn oath,
and entered into a covenant with you',
declares the Sovereign Lord, 'and you
became mine' (Ezekiel 16:8—and the whole
chapter).

For Paul, mutual love and honour between
husbands and wives becomes a wonderful
reflection of the union between Christ and of
believers:

[W]e are members of [Christ's] body. For
this reason a man will leave his father and
mother and be united to his wife, and the
two will become one flesh. This is a
profound mystery—but I am talking about
Christ and the church (Ephesians 5:30-32).

There are, we might say, hidden depths to the
consummation of the man-woman relationship in marriage—for God has privileged it to
bear the image of the bond between Christ,
our head and saviour, and the church which is
his body. This we know by revelation alone: it

is one of the 'open secrets' published in the gospel.

A fundamental structure

It is important to note the fundamental structural role played in the Bible by the God-given differentiation between man and woman, and the complementarity of their sexualities. It is not too much to say that these are assumed throughout God's Word in Scripture. As a consequence, we find a sharp contrast between the Bible's approach and the one adopted in many contemporary discussions, including a number of church reports. The latter often start with a celebration of God's gift of sexuality in general terms, and only then go on to ask how this common sexuality may be properly expressed amid the options on offer in today's sexual free market. The assumption seems to be that there is an undetermined sexuality which may find an outlet in different forms of sexual behaviour. The only question is which forms are legitimate.

The Bible, on the other hand, starts with heterosexuality—and assumes it as the God-given norm throughout. The sexuality which God's Word in Scripture invites us to celebrate is from first to last the distinct sexual identities of male and female created for each other. The failure to begin where the Bible begins is responsible for much of the confusion abroad today. Even in the churches, debate too often adopts as a basis, not the biblical revelation, but assumptions commonly accepted in contemporary society. The Bible knows nothing of an undifferentiated, indeterminate sexuality, waiting, so to speak, to fix its sense of direction, its orientation: male for male or for female, or for both? female for male or for female, or for both? adult for adult or for child? Christians who take their bearings from God's Word in Scripture, as the churches profess to, cannot view these options as morally equivalent to each other, as though sexual ethics were to be settled on a consumer-led, free-choice model.

Before we move on, we must take this argument one step further. The sexual matching of male and female, which Christian tradition has always seen as rooted in God's ordering of the world he made, is embodied (literally) in the respective anatomies of man and woman. To put it bluntly, the penis and the vagina are 'made for' each other, in a way that is patently not true for the penis and any other orifice in the female body, let alone the male body, or for the vagina and any other protuberance of the male—or female—body. That is to say, God's creative design for male and female to mate with each other is not airy-fairy theory, but a basic Christian belief that is borne out in the sort of human beings we are. It is a truth incarnated in our very flesh and blood.

Disordered sexuality

Why then, it may be asked, is there so much sexual confusion and disorder in most Western societies today? The Christian faith has one sombre response to this question which is as old as Christianity itself—and as true to human experience in every age. It is simply this: the whole of humankind is 'fallen'; a deep-seated fault-line is inherent in all human beings, and one—but only one—manifestation of it is the disruption of sexual order. The distorting bias which runs through all human existence, even at its noblest and most altruistic, and indeed at its most religious, has damaged us in every aspect of our behaviour and relationships. All forms of sexual activity which deviate from the biblical norm represent a failure to live sexually as God intended.

In fact, as is made clear in Romans chapters 1-2, the diagnosis cuts more deeply still. It finds the 'fallenness' of humanity not only in what we do, but also in the kinds of persons we are—greedy, aggressive, self-seeking and self-centred, lustful. Human nature is corrupted at its heart—and Christian teaching dares to claim that the most serious symptom of this is our failure to love and honour God as we ought.

Example and teaching of Jesus

Jesus was known as the friend of 'sinners'—with 'sinner' meaning not so much all without exception as those who lived a flagrantly immoral life or followed a disreputable way of earning their living; 'sinner' might also denote those who did not live in accordance with strict rabbinic laws. He attracted many whom the strictly religious (represented by the Pharisees) despised and excluded. He was impatient of legalism. He was also, we are told, non-judgmental; he treated the woman caught committing adultery in a remarkably accepting manner. Moreover, he said nothing about homosexuality and showed little interest in sexual misdemeanours.

However, we should avoid the pitfall of a selective reading of the Gospels. In the Sermon on the Mount, Jesus did not relax or cancel the Seventh Commandment, 'You shall not commit adultery'; rather he strengthened it by extending its scope to cover also the lustful heart (Matthew 5:27-28). As we have seen, he did not tell the woman of John 8:3-11 that adultery was not sinful; in fact he told her to stop sinning, while himself refusing to condemn her to the punishment decreed by the Mosaic law. The Rich Young Ruler who sought the way to eternal life was reminded by Jesus first of all of the commandments (Mark 10:7-20). And when challenged about the grounds for divorce, Jesus undoubtedly took a stricter line than the law of Moses had done (such that in the earliest centuries of the church divorce was not allowed at all).

The too prevalent one-sided picture of Jesus that we are evaluating tends to stress that he accepted people unconditionally just as they were and that he 'affirmed' them in their self-worth and dignity. Sometimes this emphasis is combined with a heavy use of sayings such as John 10:10: 'I have come that the sheep may have life, and have it more abundantly', with the implication that the new life of which the Jesus of John's Gospel repeatedly speaks were an enhanced version of ordinary human life shorn of its restrictions.

Jesus Forgave Sinners

Yet the core message of Jesus was not 'I love you and accept you just as you are', but 'The time is fulfilled and the kingdom of God is at hand: repent and believe in the gospel' (Mark 1:15). Self-denial and taking up the cross must be the marks of those who would become his disciples (Mark 8:34-38). Jesus 'affirmed' no one in a life of sinning. He did not' affirm' the adulteress in her adulterous existence but only in her readiness to have done with it ('Go now and leave your life of sin', John 8:11, cf. 4:17f.). Jesus did not 'affirm' sinners but forgave them which proved to be in the eyes of some Jewish theologians one of his most provocative and contentious actions (Mark 2:5-12). So when an unnamed woman lavished extravagant devotion on Jesus, it was because she knew how greatly she had been forgiven (Luke 7:44-50)!

There is, then, in the Gospels no evidence that Jesus adopted a distinctively relaxed or accepting attitude in marital and sexual ethics. He undoubtedly highlighted the heart rather than the external act alone, but why? 'For from within, out of a person's heart, come evil thoughts, sexual immorality, theft, murder, adultery, greed...' (Mark 7:21-22). And he undoubtedly accented love more than law, but not love against law—rather love as that which will fulfil the deepest intention of God's law, from the heart, instead of being content with mere outward conformity.

And if Jesus had nothing to say about homosexuality, that should not surprise us. As we have already noted, Israel was among those cultures where homosexuality was not a common occurrence. It became an issue only as Israelites intermingled with Canaanites and later with the Greek world. All the evidence suggests that Jesus' silence about homosexuality has nothing to do with indifference to it in ethical terms.

'Love is all that matters'

The appeal to love as the overarching ethical criterion, superseding the specifics of legal enactments, has been a feature of many modern restatements of Christian ethics. Sometimes in its support it has misquoted Augustine as advocating 'Love and do what you wish'. In fact, Augustine was far from teaching that love alone should determine how one should act ('So long as you love, you can do what you like'—to express it at its most provocative). The phrase should be translated more like, 'Make sure you love, and then do what you intend to do'. Augustine was concerned to reconcile a heart of love with external acts that were punitive or severe. In the context, the words justified the coercion of religious dissenters: provided one loved them, one could impose restrictions or sanctions upon them. So long as a parent loves a child, he or she may discipline the child. Love, then, is the essential disposition that must inform the restraints or constraints of law.

Understanding 'God is Love'

Sometimes the impression is given that the affirmation 'God is love' is absolute, timeless truth, whereas moral norms, such as 'you shall not commit adultery' and 'you shall not covet your neighbour's wife' are relative and culture-bound—in these cases belonging to a patriarchal society, for instance. This account of things is too simple by half. The whole of Scripture is given to us in specific historical contexts and languages. As a truth claiming biblical authority, 'God is love' is no less historically relative than 'you shall not lie with a man as with a woman'. In this statement 'God' denotes not any being we choose to give the name to, but only the God revealed in a particular setting, whether that be the Judaeo-Christian revelation as a whole, or the New Testament, or only 1 John (where the particular assertion occurs, at 4:8 and 4:16). Likewise 'love' here means not a romanticized sentiment, nor sexual intercourse, nor do-goodism, but only love as defined or embodied in the specific context, where God's love is revealed in sending his Son to die as the atoning sacrifice for our sins (1 John 4:10). This sacrificial love of God is always entirely 'gift-love', unlike human love which is invariably, in the final analysis, 'need-love'.

In John's First Epistle it is not human love that fixes the meaning of God's love, but rather the reverse; true love is modelled for us by God himself (3:16, 4:10, 4:19). And in this context it is a divine love that distinguishes between 'the children of God' and 'the children of the devil' (3:10); and it is a love that teaches that the true children of God do not continue in sin (3:9, 5:18). Fellowship with the God who is love is incompatible with 'walking in darkness'—for in that fellowship with God 'the blood of Jesus, his Son, purifies us from all sin' (1:6-7).

Let me repeat this point for clarity's sake. If we wish to claim biblical justification for believing that 'God is love' (rather than, say, relying on our own insight or a general religious consensus), there is no escaping the fact that we find the phrase in a particular document (1 John), in a particular language (Greek), in a particular era (the later first century), and in a particular historical setting (which is not easy to ascertain for this document). If we reflect this kind of divine love, we will not hate our brothers or sisters (3:15, 4:20), but sin is defined, not as love-lessness, but as lawlessness (3:4), and there is no knowledge of God without obedience to his commandments (2:3-5). This is the context to which 'God is love' belongs, and within which its implications are to be sought.

More generally too, we may say that love, as a pattern or norm of Christian or church behaviour, is not presented to us in the New Testament as dispensing with or excluding specific standards-laws, duties, respons-ibilities and the like. According to John's Gospel Jesus taught:

> If you obey my commands, you will remain in my love, just as I have obeyed my Father's commands and remain in his love... You are my friends if you do what I command... This is my command: Love each other (John 15:10, 14, 17).

Homosexual orientation

There is another major objection to the conviction of most Christians (shared by most Jews and Muslims) that homosexual activity is unacceptable in the sight of God. This objection argues that the Bible is wholly irrelevant because it is out of date. The argument goes that none of the biblical writers—nor indeed anyone until the last century or so—knew the difference between homosexual acts and the homosexual orientation which inclines some people 'naturally' towards sexual fulfilment with persons of the same sex. On this view, for certain people an homosexual inclination is 'given', not chosen by them.

From time to time reports in the media tell of scientific advances which support this claim, such as the discovery of 'a homosexual gene'. Thus since our 'nature' is given to us rather than determined by us, it cannot be wrong for us to act in accordance with it. Indeed, we may believe that God made us this way. This is a serious objection, on which several points need to be made in response.

1. It is undoubtedly true that some individuals—recent surveys in several countries put the number around one to two per cent of the population[3]—understand themselves to be exclusively homosexual in orientation. It is not a credible claim that all homosexual

---

[3] Recent medical research suggests the true percentage is 0.1% or one in every thousand, excluding bi-sexuals.

activity is indulged in by free choice, as it were, on the part of people who are normally heterosexual—though some certainly is, more among women than men.

2. On the question of the causes or origins of such a homosexual identity, there is no agreement among the experts. The case for a genetic basis, with one's homosexuality inherited from one's parents by procreation, is not proven. And even if genetic causation were established, the further question would remain of its relation to the effects of one's early development, particularly in terms of one's relationship to one or both of one's parents. Several studies have found the causes of homosexuality in upbringing rather than genetic make-up. Research continues.

3. But we must place no weight on the present lack of an agreed scientific explanation, as though we were taking refuge in gaps in our knowledge to invoke spiritual or moral factors. For science does not dictate to Christian theology or ethics. It may well throw up new problems for Christians to grapple with or throw fresh light on an old problem, but advances in theory or application do not decide ethical issues. We are more than our genes! Abortion does not become acceptable merely because improved

health care has made it infinitely safer for an expectant mother than it used to be.

4. It may be valid to distinguish between homosexual orientation as not sinful or wrong, and the wilful expression of that orientation in overt actions. After all, the fact that most people are 'made' to find sexual fulfilment with persons of the opposite sex does not, according to Christian teaching, justify extra-marital sex, such as adultery or resort to prostitutes. We will return to this point.

5. Christian doctrine contains a framework within which to understand not only acts but also persons' constitutions. The distinction between the world as God the Creator intended it to be and the world as it is—fallen, sinful and subject to corruption—is enormously relevant. Homosexual orientation, although not morally reprehensible, is nevertheless one of the myriad symptoms of the sickness plaguing human society. It must be understood within the context of creation-and-fall that comprehends all of life. We receive and enjoy the world as God's gift, and we rejoice in the many-splendoured richness of human life. Yet it is too simple by half to regard God as 'affirming' without qualification the realities of human existence, as

though his world were not shot through with the fault-lines of our sinfulness, which must deeply distress him.

6. There is another important reason why we cannot allow the fact of homosexual orientation of itself to determine our Christian ethics. It is because we do not recognize the right of every innate disposition to express itself in outward behaviour. We insist on assessing each instance on its own merits, and refuse to let the mere fact of a person's 'nature' settle the issue. Some paedophiles lay claim to a powerful inclination (to find sexual satisfaction only with boys) that is as much 'given' as anyone's 'natural' inclination. Others may regard paedophilia as a pathological condition (and who knows whether it will not be found to have a genetic base?), but for a particular individual it may seem inescapably 'given' rather than chosen. The same might be said of other apparently irresistible inward compulsions, such as kleptomania. The point is that merely being a kleptomaniac is not normally held to excuse a person's stealing.

7. Finally, it is not a particular orientation or 'nature', whether homosexual or of any other kind, that gives us our identity That consists in our humanity, our being human persons—as Christians would add, made in

the image of God, whether we are male or female. This is the true dignity that we must recognize and respect in all our fellow human beings. This is a very important point, especially for our acceptance in Christ. At the deepest level, none of us is 'a homosexual' or 'a heterosexual', but a human being, male or female, called to the redemption of human life in Christ. Acceptance, then, can no more be grounded in one person's 'gay identity' than in another's heterosexuality.

An Essential Distinction

Some may feel that distinguishing between homosexual orientation (as not a matter of personal guilt) and homosexual acts (as sinful) is ultimately unhelpful. What it amounts to is loving the sinner and hating the sin—which may be asking the impossible (and hence encouraging hostility towards homosexual persons) or suggesting an unreal distinction between what a person is and what a person does. Are the two not intimately, even inseparably, bound together? Yet the distinction, even if it lends itself too easily to glib slogans, is surely inescapable in all Christian ethics and pastoral ministry. It is in fact part of the argument of this chapter that we begin to think in a satisfactorily Christian way about homosexuality only when we view it not as a unique challenge but in terms of broader Christian beliefs and principles. Indeed it could be said that 'hating the sin but loving the sinner' is not only a healthy and compassionate guideline for Christian love in action but even expresses the heart of God himself. It may sound simplistic, but it sums up the holy passion that drove God in his love for sinful humanity to go to the uttermost to free us from our sins. It goes right to the heart of the gospel. The Bible has many ways of speaking of God's separating sinners from their sins.

It is true that in God there is no distinction between act and being. God's true being is not hidden behind his acts, or different from them. His supreme action-the sending of his Son to redeem sinful humankind-perfectly and fully expresses and embodies his divine nature. But this cannot be simply applied to human persons-for two reasons.

In the first place, we are all fallen creatures. To harmonize our actions to our fallen nature (our 'old humanity', as Paul describes it) would merely give vent to our sinfulness. And secondly, the unity of act and being that we must seek is the conformity of our lives to the 'new being' that is ours in Christ. It is to this 'new humanity', not to our own inner nature, that we must shape all we do.

Resisting Social Pressures

It is proving difficult in our society to treat homosexuality except as a special case. One reason is the success of the gay lobby in mobilising media support for its cause, and likewise of the Christian gay and lesbian movement in the churches. Another reason is the tendency of grass-roots public opinion, fed by the advertising industry, to reduce moral basics to a matter of sexual behaviour.

It is important for Christians to be aware of other ways in which social trends impinge upon, or complicate, the task of working out how Christians should live. The free expression of one's sexual appetites is widely regarded today almost as a basic human right—one of the blessings of an emancipated secular or liberal society. To repress or curb sexual instincts is thought to be almost unhealthy, and certainly abnormal. Against such a backcloth, the voluntary commitment to lifelong virginity or celibacy ('chastity', in one of its traditional senses)[4] is liable to seem weird or cranky, whereas in Christian

---

[4] See Chapter 6.

teaching from Jesus and Paul onwards it is a noble Christian vocation.

It should not go unnoticed that some who are arguing for the acceptability of homosexual activity (within appropriate limits) are also arguing likewise for hetero-sexual intercourse outside the setting of marriage in which alone, according to age-old Christian teaching, it properly belongs. By the same token, it should not be surprising if those who see no reason to depart from the church's heterosexual ethic are not persuaded by the case for recognizing homosexual behaviour. Even if the long-term cohabitation of unmarried partners who are exclusively faithful to each other may necessitate fresh thought about the essence of marriage (after all, such a relationship often legally constitutes 'common-law' marriage), this would be a minor adjustment compared with the revolution involved in overthrowing the normative character of male-and-female complementarity in Scripture.

Unanswered Questions

There are many questions that this chapter has not attempted to deal with. The relation between (Christian) morality and (public) law is one of them. Christians are now a shrinking minority in Britain, despite having national churches in Scotland and England. It is no easy task to determine how much influence Christian conviction should seek to exercise on legislation in a largely secular society.

Another question left untouched here is that of church discipline, as it applies to members or ministers. At least in the Reformed (especially Presbyterian) tradition, church discipline is a pastoral function, designed to correct only in order to recover. So there can be no automatic carryover from believing that homosexual activity is wrong to determining how best to deal with lapses of this sort. Yet churches in all traditions have always held to higher expectations of ordained personnel, both in beliefs and behaviour, than of members at large.

The gospel and church for homosexuals

Perhaps the hardest challenge to the churches will not be holding fast to the conviction cannot approve of same-sex sexuality—in spite of the crystal clarity of the Scriptures. Rather the most searching task will be to build communities of spiritual warmth where struggling individuals will find Christian forgiveness and re-creation.

The gay movement's toughest challenge is not the recasting of Christian beliefs but the spiritual renewal of our congregations, so that week by week we may love and nurture towards wholeness people suffering from sexual and emotional brokenness of many kinds. Can the church be a living embodiment of the gospel?

Epilogue

Is there any response that Christian fellowships, university Christian Unions and other groupings of believers should be making today to the massive assault which is being brought against the traditional biblical standards of morality? Ought those of us who profess to follow Jesus Christ to be taking any clear action to stem the floodtide of increasing sexual chaos? Are the Bible's standards still relevant today? And as we move forward in the twenty-first century, is Christianity still a force to be reckoned with?

There are several ways in which those who profess the Christian faith can react to the sexual revolution which is going on all around us. One would be to allow our standards slowly and imperceptibly to be eroded as the shadow of the world's hand moves silently over the church's life. It cannot be denied to that to some extent that is already happening. There are congregations and gatherings of believers where immorality is openly tolerated among leaders. There are fellowships in which extra-marital relationships are no longer closely guarded secrets. And there is an increasingly obvious change in moral attitudes among many who claim to be Christians. The constant, inexorable deluge of media propaganda is relentlessly taking its toll of many believers' attitudes.

This erosion of biblical morality within the churches requires to be recognized for what it is—a threat ultimately to the church's very existence (see Revelation 3:2–3).

Another possible response by the church is to act as if nothing needs to be done and no changes are necessary. Many express the opinion that in time the tide will turn and there will be a swing back to more traditional attitudes. There are many sincere believers who voice this pious, but improbable, hope. The ostrich likewise hopes danger will disappear if it hides its head in the sands!

No. The church must change. Christians must adopt a clear, deliberate strategy to defend the validity and truth of the Bible's teaching on morality and they must also actively promote the values which are offered to us in Christ. The following suggestions may appear deceptively simple but they could have profound effects for good.

First, biblical teaching on morality should be explicitly taught from Christian pulpits, in Bible Classes, Christian Unions, for every age and stage. It is no use hoping that young people will somehow 'pick up' the Scripture's reasoning and values. The influence of society and the media is powerful, constant, explicit and compelling, appealing as it does to fallen human nature. It can only be countered by firm, clear teaching which cannot be mis-understood.

I am not suggesting the old moralistic ranting about morality be revived, but rather that 'bridges' be built from the 'then and there' of Scripture to the 'here and now' of contemporary society. In other words, the problems need to be spelt out. The provision of God for our benefit needs to be lovingly shown. The consequences of disobedience need to be explained. All this without embarrassment but clearly taught in a relevant, realistic way.

There is a note to be sounded which is seldom heard. It is that close friendship need not have a sexual orientation. It is increasingly assumed by our generation that where there is same-sex friendship, there must inevitably be a sexual undertone. C.S. Lewis deplored this attitude in his book *The Four Loves*. But his warning appears to have gone unnoticed and unheeded. Christians need to recover the concept and reality of wholesome friendship as exemplified in the relationship between David and Jonathan. I know that today aspersions are cast that theirs *must have been* a homosexual love. But in Israel such practices were abhorred, while chaste friendship was exalted. Those who teach in Christian fellowships must eloquently and consistently affirm the honour of the chaste friendship between Christians of the same sex.

That such teaching is not being given at present is self-evident. This is the first response that is urgently called for.

Second, the family needs to be powerfully affirmed on two distinct levels. There is the microcosm of the nuclear family. There is also the macrocosm of the Christian family. Unwittingly, the church herself has been the agent of disintegration of the family at both levels. Much church life divides members of the fellowship on the grounds of both age and gender. The accommodation churches often provide is designed exactly for the purpose of separating the family members off into various little groups. But the church should be a great uniting agent bringing her members together in a manner that spans all barriers of age and gender, not least in her times of worship on the Lord's Day.

Those who have the oversight of Christian congregations of all denominations ought to be working hard at promoting family values for each home and for the wider fellowship.

Third, each church should also be working to provide pastoral care for those in special need of moral help. Too often, when a brother or sister makes a moral slip, the response is one of condemnation and isolation. Too often, there is a lack of understanding, compassion and ongoing support, especially for those who repeatedly fall.

In this regard, few congregations (or groups of congregations) make any provision for those who, through no fault of their own, find their sexual orientation is not 'straight'. Many a homosexual has suffered for years in silence, enduring unthinkable anguish and frustration, longing for someone with whom to share their secret and who will offer loving friendship and patient support.

I am convinced it ought to be openly known that within each area of Christian churches there is the equivalent of a 'help-line' for homosexuals who are struggling with their lonely burden. It would be in the hands of some person(s), suitably trained and spiritually mature, set apart for this ministry, and whose confidentiality is assured. Weekly intimation sheets which many Christian congregations now have should give such a 'help line' telephone number.

Some smaller fellowships may not be able to resource this kind of provision. But groups of congregations working together should be able to work out a practicable scheme and so offer help to those who without such support may well be enticed by the treacherous seductions of a godless society and find warmer friendship and acceptance in a gay pub or club.

In all of this, our great Exemplar is Christ himself. The church is his Body. The local community too seldom sees the radiant face of Christ, or hears his gracious voice, or experiences the warmth of his love. We will only be true to our holy calling when Christ is not only among us, but when we as the family of God actually become 'Jesus Christ' in our communities. And that can only be when holiness, compassion and love emanate from our common life together. May God grant that this will be increasingly so for his glory.

DCS